To Kill a Mockingbird

Novel Unit

Publisher's Note: This book was made by humans. -- if you find errors or typos – please let us know and they will be immediately researched and, if appropriate, fixed.

Table of Contents

If you would like to see student page for each activity in this novel unit – please email Elizabeth at elizabeth@luckyjenny.com.

Free instructional Powerpoints to go with this and other units are available at: http://www.luckyjenny.com/free-curriculum.html

A Quick and Dirty Guide to TKAM (To Kill A Mockingbird)

Motifs

A motif is any element, subject, idea or concept that is present throughout an entire body of literature. Motifs are extremely noticeable and play an important role in defining the nature of the story, the course of events and the fabric of the literary piece.

Motif	How Motif is Linked to Mockingbird
Life in a Small Town	Life in a small town is seen as wholesome and pure – rife with small-town values. Life is a small two is seen as slower, less sophisticated and good. Small town life is often seen as the center-point of the American Dream. The small town of Maycomb is used to offset the forces of good and evil that seethe through the plot. If one looks closely, all of the good of small-town life and values is countered by underlying darkness – Scout ridiculed by Bob Ewell for her pageant costume contrasted by the town pulling together in other instances.
Gothic	The South highlights the forces of good and evil that weave through *To Kill a Mockingbird*. These gothic takes add an intensity to the novel and created a clouded, heavy feel. These elements include the strange snowfall, the fire at Miss Maudie's home, the superstition surrounding Boo Radley, the dark night of the Halloween party. These gothic elements foreshadow what is to come.

Themes

Themes are the underlying meanings of literary work. A theme may be stated or implied.

Themes	*To Kill a Mockingbird* Themes
Good vs. Evil	The notion that good and evil exist on the same pendulum is evident throughout *To Kill a Mockingbird*. This theme is explored through the novel's rich characters and is evident in the growth from the innocence of childhood to a more worldly and grown-up view of the world as Scout and Jem experience evil and must learn to live with and process the results of hatred, prejudice and ignorance.

The ability to adapt to the perception of good vs. evil and its simultaneous presence are essential for survival as depicted by the fact that neither Tim Robinson nor Boo Radley could process or adapt to the evil and were destroyed.

Additionally, Scout never loses her inner faith in humanity, as trying as the situation gets, she adapts her view and grows; whereas, Jem's loses faith and is negatively affected.

Atticus Finch is the novel's window into the idea that everyone possesses qualities of good and evil and the human capacity for goodness should never be lost in that realization. He emphasizes that for survival it is necessary to concentrate on the good and to try to see the world through the lens of others.

As the novel progresses, Atticus slowly brings Scout to this realization. This transfer between Atticus and Scout helps ensure that as she does grow, and innocence is lost, she does not become cynical. |

Morality	In a very real sense, *To Kill a Mockingbird* is about the journey of Scout as she grows in relation to morality and the perception of morality. This theme manifests itself particularly in the relationship between Atticus and his children. The hypocrisy of adulthood and the irony of teacher and adult commitment further highlight the divide between morality in words vs. morality in application.
Social Inequality	The social structure of Maycomb county underlies every action in the novel and serves as a point of confusion for the children. The implications of the social hierarchy are complicated and destructive.

Symbols

A symbol is literary device containing multiple layers of meaning, usually concealed at first, and representative of several other aspects, concepts or traits than those that are visible in what is literal, thus, symbolism is using an object or action that means something more than its literal meaning.

Symbols	Symbolism
Mockingbirds	The titled mockingbirds are symbolic of innocence destroyed as the mockingbird represents everything that is harmless. The characters themselves can be labeled mockingbirds in that Jem, Tom Robinson, Boo, Dill and Mr. Raymond are destroyed as evil swells and overtakes them. The comparison Mr. Underwood makes, after Tom Robinson is shot, draws a direct connection to the titled mockingbirds :…the senseless slaughter of songbirds." Later, Scout remarks that hurting Boo Radley is akin to "…shootin' a mockingbird. Another exampled comes from Miss Maude to Scout "Mockingbirds…sing their hearts out for us. That's why it's a sin to kill a mockingbird." As Boo is a mockingbird in Lee's novel, so too is Atticus in that he was known to be a role model of fairness and honesty, yet he is chastised for taking on the case of a black man.
Boo Radley	As *To Kill a Mockingbird* progresses and the children transcend innocence, Boo Radley is a symbolic measure of that growth. His humanization in the eyes of Scout, as the novel progresses, illustrates a compassion and understanding that is good in scout. Boo is Radley is the symbol of good in the novel.
The Mad Dog	The mad dog is, at the same time, a representation of what is safe and known but can morph into something hostile and dangerous. The community of Maycomb is safe, until Mayelle Ewell is attacked and then the safe and abiding townspeople become dangerous, mad beings.

A Quick and Dirty Guide to Literary Elements

The literary devices and nuances of *To Kill a Mockingbird* should be taught through the course of this unit as examples become present. Introduce the elements, as they relate to the novel, all at once at the beginning of the unit, after the non-fiction piece, as it is helpful and provides a basis for student understanding.

The Basics:

Voice: First person narrative. Scout is older reflecting back on the story. This approach adds an air of innocence that grips the reader and enables a dual look at the events of Maycomb. Most of the events are told from the lens of a child, however, Scout being older and removed from the events allows the introjection of the occasional adult perspective. *Mr. Underwood didn't talk about miscarriages of justice, he was writing so children could understand. Mr. Underwood simply figured it was a sin to kill cripples, be they standing, sitting, or escaping.* The child Scout doesn't understand "miscarriages of justice" but the adult does.

Genre: *Coming of age*. Even though Scout is young, she grows in her view of the world as well as in her ability to act as a lady.

Southern Gothic: There is a haunted house, with a haunted being – the Radley Place and Boo Radley. There is also darkness and evil – courtesy of Bob Ewell.

Tone: innocent, naïve, ironic, nostalgic and even critical

Plot Analysis:

- **Exposition:** The Finches have lived for generations in the small town of Maycomb in Alabama. They fit into the community and have many friends. *To Kill a Mockingbird* is set in Alabama in the 1930s where racism was the norm and while Atticus is not a racist, and is raising his children to be the same, his loved ones and friends are racist, but he is prone to forgiving the shortcomings of others.
- **Conflict:** Almost all men are created equal – providing they are white and male. Yes, there are undertones of sexism as well as the overt conflict of racism in this novel. A conflict arises when Atticus, father of Scout and Jem, is charged with defending a black man in a community that does not value true equality.
- **Climax:** The prejudice of the community triumphs over good, and the Finches, only Scout's innocence remains – even through the trial and subsequent events.
- **Falling Action:** Tom Robinson is shot and Jem has trouble with the inequity of the situation. Bob Ewell attacks Jem and Scout in the night and is killed by the mysterious Boo Radley

Main Characters	
Scout Finch	Jean Louise Finch, aka Scout, is the protagonist and narrator of To Kill a Mockingbird. Over the course of the novel, Scout grows from six to nine-years-old. She lives in Maycomb, Alabama with her father, Atticus, and her brother Jem. Scout is a tomboy and has deep faith in humanity, that while tested over the course of the novel by the prejudice and even hatred that surface as the result of her father, an attorney, defending a black man, it does not fully diminish. Scout grows to face the evil, without ignoring human goodness.
Jem Finch	Scout's all-American boy brother. He is four years older than Scout and even as he grows and separates himself from his sister – he remains her protector and friend. Jem is affected by the hatred and injustice that result from the trial and his father defending a black man and does not escape the events with the same buoyancy as his sister Scout seems to.
Atticus Finch	Scout and Jem's widowed father. He has a strong sense of morality and justice and seems committed to racial equality – rare in his town. Even though he strives for racial equality, he lives in the world he exists and there are inconsistencies about racial interaction, that while unjust, he accepts. He agrees to defend a black man against the charge of rape.
Boo Radley	Boo is a neighbor mysterious recluse who plays on the imaginations of Scout, Jem and their friend Dill. He is the symbol of purity and goodness. He is a mockingbird – even though he is, at first, surrounded by a foreboding, gothic darkness. Having been damaged by his religiously zealous father, Arthur *Boo* Radley emerges as a symbol of innocence and goodness.
Bob Ewell	Bob is the patriarch of one of Maycomb's poorest and lowest families. He is dark, mean and evil. He is filled with racial prejudice and is symbolic of the reason achieving even a modicum of racial equality, in the South, was difficult.
Dill Harris	The Finch children's summer friend. Dill is a fun child with an active imagination and a sense of innocence that helps to deepen the theme of *innocence lost* as the novel progresses.
Aunt Alexandra	Atticus' sister and the keeper of the family's Finch Landing property. As the novel progresses and the story evolves, Aunt Alexandra comes to live with Atticus and the children to add a feminine influence. She is a typical Southern *lady*, she is proud of her status and heritage and wants Scout and Jem to be and feel the same way.
Miss Maudie	An old friend of Atticus' and the Finches' neighbor. She is a widow who is not afraid to speak her mind. She is a good friend of Jem and Scout and possesses Atticus' sense of justice.
Calpurnia	The Finch family cook. She helps raise the children with a stern hand. She is the link between the white and black world as Scout grows and becomes more exposed to the happenings of both worlds – notices subtle differences in Calpurnia's behavior.
Mayella Ewell	The accuser of Tom Robinson. She is the nineteen-year-old, illiterate daughter of Bob Ewell. She is so afraid of her father that lies about the incident with Tom Robinson.
Tom Robinson	The black man accused of rape. He is symbolic of innocence demolished by hate and prejudice. He is a mockingbird.

Name: _____ Date: _____

The Character and Theme Link (CCSS RL.2)

Choose four characters, link each to one to a theme of *To Kill a Mockingbird*, and site examples of this link through the character's actions, lack of actions, statements, decisions and/or quotes.

Character	Theme	Example
		Page number _____
		Page number _____
		Page number _____
		Page number _____

Activities

Fluency and Comprehension Practice

Differentiation: Students struggling with comprehension and fluency will benefit from reading chapter summaries after nightly readings. While the summaries benefit all students, you may or may not want to assign them to the entire class. The summaries make a great addition to interactive notebook pages and are useful for test prep. Complete this assignment before chapter quizzes to help students better understand the novel content.

Instruction for Fluency Practice For a Group or a Whole Class

Increasing student fluency proficiency through literature is an engaging way to help students move from dragging themselves across endless pages of text – to truly enjoying the written word. Practicing fluency proficiency is just as important for the reluctant high school reader as it is for struggling beginning readers. The following techniques, designed to move students to reading
fluency, are research-based and use highly effective instructional strategies.

The fluency passages after these instructions are *To Kill a Mockingbird* chapter summaries. They are written to help students understand the text. Following each passage are comprehension questions. For some groups of students it is easier for them to enjoy what they are reading and get through the chapters in the book if they read the chapter fluency summaries first. This helps both confidence and comprehension.

Students may read in pairs and time each other or read softly aloud into a computer, phone or other recording device, calculate their words per minute and then playback their recording.

Instructions for Reading Alone:

1. Explain what fluency is: Fluency is the rate and ease at which we read. The flow of reading. This activity will take about ten minutes and will help us all learn to read more fluently...to help your reading flow smoothly. To practice fluency we are going to read a short passage, figure out how many words we are each reading per minute and then answer some questions about what we have just read.

2. Explain how to calculate Words Per Minute:
   *   Set the timer
   *   Read the passage
   *   Put an x over words you don't know
   *   Mark the spot you're at when the timer dings after two minutes
   *   Finish the passage
   *   Count how many words read in two minutes
   *   Divide by 2
   *   Subtract any wrong words
   *   = words per minutes

   > Total Words Read: 150
   > Divide by 2: 75
   > Minus errors: -4
   > = WPM 71 WPM

Instructions for Fluency in Pairs: Same instructions as reading alone – only one student tracks WPM and errors while the other reads. I prefer to do Fluency in pairs.

Name: _____ **Date:** _____ # _____

To Kill a Mockingbird – Chapter 1

The narrator of *To Kill a Mockingbird* is an innocent small town girl nicknamed	14
Scout. The novel opens with Scout explaining an old story about the broken arm of	29
her big brother Jem. Through this story, the reader learns that her family fled	43
England to escape religious persecution and settled on a farm on the banks of the	57
Alabama River. The farm was successful for her grandparents and enabled Scout's	69
father, Atticus Finch, to become a lawyer in the small town of Maycomb. Scout's	83
father has two siblings, a sister who runs the farm and a brother who went to	99
Boston to become a doctor.	104
The novel takes place between Scout's sixth and ninth years; however, as the	117
narrator, she is retelling the story from later in life and the voice fluctuates between	132
a child's and that of an adult remembering events of days gone by. The voice of	148
innocence dominates the novel's tone and drives the central plot, allowing the reader	161
insight into Scout, her family and life in Alabama in the 1930s.	173
Maycomb is in the grips of the Great Depression, but Atticus does well as a	188
small town lawyer. He and his two children, Scout and Jem, live in town with their	204
cook, Calpurnia, who helps raise them. Calpurnia is an old black woman who serves	218
as the mother figure and disciplinarian for Scout and her brother. Calpurnia is the	232
bridge between the divided black and white worlds that exist in Maycomb. Scout	245
has an interesting perception of Calpurnia which evolves as the story progresses. At	258
first, the child sees the older woman as less than human, strict and mighty, Scout	273
does not initially recognizes that Calpurnia is tough on her because she loves her	287
and wants what is best for her.	294
The plot begins when Scout's bother Jem is ten and she is six and they	309
encounter a young boy, Dill, Charles Baker Harris, who is in town for the summer,	324
staying with his aunt, Miss Rachel Haverford. Dill is smart and talkative, except	337
when it comes to his father. He and the Finches become fast friends. Dill eventually	353
convinces the Finches that they should attempt to lure their mysterious neighbor,	365
Boo Radley, out of his rundown house. No one has seen Boo outside in years and	381
Scout tells how Boo got in trouble years before and, as a result, his father made him	398
a prisoner of the home. Some of the townspeople say Boo is crazy and that his father	415
would not commit him. Boo lives with his brother Nathan. When Dill finally dares	429
Jem to go over and touch the house, Jem comes back quickly claiming to have seen	445
a shutter move.	448
The first chapter highlights the youthful innocence and carefree world of the	460
Finch children and their friend Dill, who is merely a Maycomb visitor; however, the	474
mystery and games surrounding Boo Radley foreshadow the darker events to come.	486
Boo is real to the children only in the superstitions that surround him. Over the	501
course of the novel Boo's gothic, allusive persona will evolve into a real person as the	517
children grow to see him through the eyes of the adult world around them.	531

Total Words Read:_____ Divided by 2: _____ Minus errors: _____ = WPM _____

Name: _____ **Date:** _____ # _____

Comprehension – Chapter 1

Summarize the passage in five sentences: _____

_____

_____

_____

_____

_____

_____

Describe one event from the chapter that is not covered in the passage: _____

_____

_____

_____

_____

_____

_____

_____

Who is Dill? _____

_____

_____

What is the Radley Place? _____

_____

_____

Who is narrating the story and who is his or her family? _____

_____

_____

Who had to touch what? _____

_____

Circle or highlight the correct answer.

1. Scout's real name is:
   a) Jem
   b) Dill
   c) Louise Jean
   d) Jean Louise

2. What is Atticus Finch's relationship to the narrator?
   a) He is her attorney
   b) He is her babysitter
   c) He is her father
   d) He is her teacher

3. *To Kill a Mockingbird* opens with Scout describing:
   a) Jem's encounter with the Radley Place
   b) Miss Stephanie Crawford
   c) Jem's broken arm
   d) Jem's relationship to Scout and Dill

4. What is the name of the town in which the Finch's live?
   a) Maybury
   b) Maycomb
   c) Calpurnia
   d) Landing

5. Who doesn't Dill want to speak about?
   a) His father
   b) Jem
   c) Scout
   d) His mother Calpurnia

6. Who does the narrator describe as a "malevolent phantom?"
   a) Scout
   b) Jem Finch
   c) Boo Radley
   d) Dill

7. Who is Miss Rachel Haverford?
   a) Dill's mother
   b) Scout's mother
   c) Dill's aunt
   d) Jem's aunt

8. According to the narrator, who was fascinated by the Radley Place?
   a) Boo
   b) Jem
   c) Miss Rachel and Miss Maudie
   d) Dill

To Kill a Mockingbird – Chapters 2 and 3

September comes; Scout gets ready to go to school for the first time and Dill	15
exits the story. Scout loves to learn and is excited about school until her teacher	30
makes her feel guilty for already knowing how to read. At recess, Scout complains	44
about her teacher to Jem, but he blows her off. Back in class, Scout's day does not	61
improve. When a classmate, Walter Cunningham, forgets his lunch, Miss Caroline	72
offers him money and says he can pay her back tomorrow. Scout knows the boy is	88
poor and that his family pays her father in vegetables and other goods and doesn't	103
have the money to repay his teacher. Scout tries to explain this to Miss Caroline,	118
only her teacher does not understand, becomes frustrated and smacks Scout's hand	130
with a ruler. This transaction shows an understanding, insight and sense of	142
compassion in Scout, that contrasts the ignorance of her teacher –the adult – in a	156
role reversal that highlights the transition Scout is making to the more mature world	170
around her.	172
During the break, Scout attacks Walter for getting her into trouble. Jem breaks	185
them up and asks Walter to join them for lunch. Back at the Finch house, Atticus	201
engages Walter in a rather grown-up conversation about farm conditions. Scout	212
criticizes Walter for the way he eats, but Calpurnia pulls her aside and tells her to	228
behave like a better hostess.	233
That afternoon, their teacher, Miss Caroline, is terrified when a bug crawls out of	247
Burris Ewell's hair. We learn that the Ewell's are even poorer and less respected	261
than the Cunninghams. Burris does not really attend school; he only goes on the	275
first day of class to abide by the law. Burris leaves the classroom, making the	290
teacher cry with his hateful words. This interchange puts the social hierarchy of	303
Maycomb into perspective and sets the stage for the adult interchange between the	316
three families.	318
That evening Scout tells Atticus that she doesn't want to go to school anymore	332
and would like him to teach her instead. Her father insists it is the law and she	349
must attend school, but he will keep reading with her if she doesn't tell her teacher	365
about it.	367
The first day of school is tumultuous for Scout by design as it highlights the	382
social hierarchy of Maycomb and sets the stage for the themes of morality, education	396
and growth. The irrational actions of an inexperienced teacher and the demands of	413
the law thrust the reader into an adult world that lacks common sense or	427
compassion and foreshadows events to come. From chapter one's world of innocent	439
childhood to the tipping point of going to school, and entering a more mature world,	464
we see Scout frustrated, but untarnished, by the often senseless actions of the	477
adults around her.	480
The social hierarchy of Maycomb evolves, and the correlation between morality	491
and social status unfolds, revealing Atticus at the top – wealthy, wise and moral,	504
while scattered about beneath him are the poor farmers, below which lie citizens like	518
the Ewells – who are portrayed as ignorant, dark and villainous.	528
Miss Caroline's rigid interpretation of the rules and her unyielding, unthinking	539
teaching methods foreshadow another public forum – the courtroom – and a like and	551
impending failure of the system.	56

Total Words Read:_____ Divided by 2: _____ Minus errors: _____ = WPM _____

Comprehension – Chapter 2 and 3

Summarize the passage in five sentences: _____

_____

_____

_____

_____

_____

_____

Describe one event from the chapter that is not covered in the passage: _____

_____

_____

_____

_____

_____

_____

Discuss what Scout explained were things she could not bother Jem with at school.

_____

_____

_____

_____

Describe why the children were skeptical of Miss Caroline when she introduced herself.

_____

_____

_____

_____

_____

Circle or highlight the correct answer.

1. In Chapter 2, when did Dill leave?
   a) Early September
   b) Late September
   c) October
   d) Come June

2. How did Scout's teacher, Miss Caroline, begin the first day of school?
   a) By reading a story about Alabama
   b) By reciting all of the students' names
   c) By reading a story about cats
   d) By reading a letter from Dill

3. Why does Miss Caroline say that Scout's father may not teacher her anymore?
   a) He doesn't know how to teach
   b) He never went to school
   c) He doesn't have a fresh mind
   d) It is her job

4. Who was to blame for Scout knowing how to write?
   a) Her father Atticus
   b) Dill
   c) Jem
   d) Calpurnia

5. What was in the molasses buckets?
   a) Lunch
   b) Supper
   c) Molasses
   d) Coins

6. Why did Scout rub Walter Cunningham's nose in the dirt?
   a) She was playing
   b) Jem told her to
   c) She thought it was too clean
   d) He got her into trouble

7. Why does Walter say he can't pass the first grade.
   a) He doesn't understand reading
   b) He has to stay out every spring to help in the fields
   c) He is always hungry
   d) He doesn't say anything at all

8. What causes Miss Caroline to get upset when they return from lunch?
   a) Scout doesn't return
   b) Walter is still hungry
   c) A bug crawls out of someone's hair
   d) She can't handle her classroom full of students

To Kill a Mockingbird -- Chapters 4, 5 and 6

As the school year progresses, Scout grows increasingly frustrated with the pace	12
of the curriculum and its lack of rigor. One day, on her way home, she passes the	30
Radley Place and finds two pieces of gum sticking out of a knothole. On the last day	47
of school she and Jem find two Indian-head pennies in the same knothole and	62
decide to keep them.	66
With the return of summer comes Dill and the fun begins again for the three	81
children. As they are playing with an old tire, Scout accidently rolls up to the Radley	97
steps. The children panic; however, the ordeal gives Jem an idea for a new game	112
called "Boo Radley" – which becomes increasingly complicated as they begin acting	123
out the life and times of the Radley family. When Atticus sees them and asks if their	140
game has anything to do with the Radley family, they lie, but the moral compasses	155
in them makes them wonder if they should, indeed, stop playing their game.	168
Through the events of Chapter 5, Dill and Jem's relationship grows, and Scout	181
feels left out. With nothing better to do, she begins to spend time with Miss Maudie	197
Atkinson, a widowed neighbor who likes to garden and bake cakes. Miss Maudie's	210
deceased husband was a childhood friend of Atticus' brother Jack and the families	223
are quite close. Miss Maudie informs Scout that Boo Radley is alive, not spooky and	238
that he was a friendly, polite child at one time. She furthers that most of the rumors	255
about him are false; however, she does relent that he is probably crazy by now	270
because his father was a religious zealot who basically scarred him for life.	283
Jem and Dill get the idea to invite Boo for ice cream, but Atticus intercepts a	299
note the boys are trying to get to Boo and tells them to leave the poor guy alone –	320
which they do until Dill is just about to leave Maycomb again. At that point, the	336
children sneak over to the Radley Place and take a peek inside. Scout goes with	351
them. When they see the shadow of a man inside, and then hear a shotgun blast off	368
behind them, they run away in fear. They make their exit under the fence by the	384
schoolyard, Jem's pants get caught and he had to leave them behind.	396
At home, neighbors have gathered. The children learn that Nathan Radley shot a	409
Negro in his yard. Atticus asks Jem where his pants are, Dill says he won them in a	427
game of cards. Jem interjects and says it was a game of matches. Jem sneaks out	434
that night and gets his pants back.	441
This chapter helps Boo Radley make the transformation from a mysterious, evil	453
creature to the human being that he is. Scout even learns, from Miss Maudie, that	468
Boo was a nice boy who was victim of his religiously fanatical father – thus Boo	483
becomes the personification of innocence lost. Miss Maudie unfolds as a strong	495
character who, like Atticus, has a sense of justice. Miss Maudie is the conscience for	510
the women of the town and a strong and steady role model for Scout.	524

Total Words Read:_____ Divided by 2: _____ Minus errors: _____ = WPM _____

Comprehension – Chapters 4, 5 and 6

Summarize the passage in five sentences: _____

_____

_____

_____

_____

_____

Describe one event from the chapter that is not covered in the passage: _____

_____

_____

_____

_____

_____

Describe how Dill and Jem's relationship grows. _____

_____

_____

_____

_____

_____

_____

Use details you remember from reading to describe Miss Maudie. _____

_____

_____

_____

_____

_____

_____

Circle or highlight the correct answer.

1. What was in the tinfoil, in the knothole, at the Radley Place?
   a) Chewing gum
   a) Candy
   b) Money
   c) Nothing

2. What was in the wedding box rings came in that Scout found in the knothole?
   a) Chewing gum
   b) An Indian head penny
   c) A polished Indian head penny
   d) Two polished Indian head pennies

3. Who rolls inside the tire?
   a) Walter
   b) Scout
   c) Jem
   d) Dill

4. What drink was a summertime ritual to enjoy in the middle of the morning?
   a) Water
   b) Coca-cola
   c) Milk
   d) Lemonade

5. Who had "crisp speech for a Maycomb County inhabitant?"
   a) Calpurnia
   b) Miss Maudie
   c) Atticus
   d) Jem

6. Miss Maudie tells Scout Boo's real name. What is it?
   a) Nathan
   b) Boo
   c) Louis
   d) Arthur

7. What did Scout see in the window of the Radley Place?
   a) Boo clear as a bell
   b) A shadow of a man with a hat on
   c) Walter and Nathan
   d) Jem

8. What did Mr. Radley scoot in his collard patch?
   a) A rabbit
   b) A person
   c) Boo
   d) Scout

Name: _____ **Date:** _____ # _____

To Kill a Mockingbird – Chapters 7 and 8

It is a new school year and Scout doesn't like school any better than she did	16
before summer began. It seems second grade will be much like first for her. Jem	31
confides in Scout that when he went back for his pants, he found them sewn and	47
folded over the fence. On the walk home from school that same day they find a ball	64
of gray twine in the knothole at the Radley Place.	74
The knothole gifts keep coming. Next in the form of soap carved into figurines	88
that look like Jem and Scout. One day, Jem and Scout go to the knothole and find	105
it's been filled with cement. When Jem asks Nathan Radley, Boo's brother about it,	120
Mr. Nathan Radley claims that the tree was dying so he had to fill the hole. Scout is	136
disappointed, but only because it is the end of the treasures. Jem, maturing, shows	151
compassion and is sad because he understands what Boo's brother is actually	163
doing: depriving Boo of his attempts to connect with the outside world. The injustice	177
Jem feels foreshadows his reaction and feelings later in the novel. This scene	190
emphasizes Scout's ability to hold onto her innocence – even as her brother grows	203
increasingly disillusioned.	205
Mrs. Radley dies and when Atticus returns home, after he goes to pay his	214
respects at the Radley house, Jem and Scout ask if he say Boo. He did not.	230
The drought of the Great Depression era receives some relief as, for the first time	245
in many years, Maycomb has a real winter. When it snows, school closes. The snow	260
is not heavy and Jem and Scout build a snow/mud man. They make it look like a	278
grouchy neighbor down the street. They do such a good job that their father makes	293
them change it. The snowman and the figurines Boo carves provide a window into	407
the intentions of each. Boo makes his as gifts for the children's pleasure, while the	422
children carve their snowman for their own mocking enjoyment of someone they	434
don't like.	436
That night, Miss Maudie's house catches fire and the townspeople, in an act of	450
compassion and solidarity, help her try to save her furniture. The firemen cannot	463
save her house. After the fire, the Finches return home and Atticus notices that	477
Scout has a blanket wrapped around her that she did not have on before. Jem	492
ascertains that it was Boo Radley who put it on her and Scout almost gets sick	518
thinking Boo was so close to her. Atticus tells them, once again, to leave Boo Radley	534
alone.	535
These early chapters are full of Boo Radley, only he never appears and the	549
reader has to infer it is Boo who fixes the pants and puts the gifts in the knothole.	567
The fire in the night and the mud mixed with the snow underscore the dramatic	582
theme of innocence threatened, but the cheerfulness of Miss Maudie, who vows to	595
rebuild after the fire, and the good Scout sees symbolize that good can triumph evil,	610
hatred, prejudice. The townspeople helping one another serve to stifle, if only	622
fleetingly, the dark gothic elements that intrude upon Maycomb and the lives of its	636
townspeople.	637
The fire serves as a tipping point in the novel and helps break the characters	652
from their childhood pursuits to the drama that unfolds as innocence is lost and the	667
adult world begins to overtake the previous cocoon from which the Finch children	680
will emerge.	682

Total Words Read:_____ Divided by 2: _____ Minus errors: _____ = WPM _____

Comprehension – Chapters 7 and 8

Summarize the passage in five sentences: _____

_____

_____

_____

_____

_____

_____

Describe one event from the chapter that is not covered in the passage: _____

_____

_____

_____

_____

_____

_____

What does Scout by: "I tried to climb into Jem's skin and walk around in it? _____

_____

_____

_____

_____

_____

What happened to Miss Maudie's house and what is her reaction to the event?

_____

_____

_____

_____

_____

_____

Circle or highlight the correct answer.

1. Jem and Scout found a ball of twine in the knothole. What color was it?
   b) gray
   d) blue
   e) green
   f) red and pink

2. What word does Scout use to describe the second grade?
   a) Fun
   b) Entertaining
   c) Grim
   d) Bad

3. What was carved into the soap?
   a) A boy and a girl
   b) Writing
   c) Nothing it was just soap
   d) A mockingbird and a tree

4. What causes Scout to cry in Chapter 7?
   a) Boo frightens her
   b) She misses Dill
   c) Someone covers up the knothole
   d) She gets in trouble

5. What was surprising about autumn turning to winter that year?
   a) The weather was the coldest it had been since 1885
   b) There was no rain at all
   c) There was no winter weather
   d) It was unseasonably hot

6. Why doesn't Miss Maude like the snow?
   a) She doesn't like the cold
   b) It will kill her azaleas
   c) She is afraid of storms
   d) Her roof is not fit to hold the weight of it.

7. Why does Atticus want Jem and Scout to change their snowman?
   a) It will hurt Boo's feelings
   b) Miss Maudie doesn't like it
   c) It looks too much like Atticus
   d) It looks too much like Mr. Avery

8. After her house burned, where did Atticus tell the children Miss Maudie would stay.
   a) With them
   b) With Miss Stephanie
   c) In a motel

To Kill a Mockingbird – Chapter 9

On the playground, Scout gets into a fight with Cecil Jacobs when he says	14
that her father defends "niggers". Scout recounts this to her father, who tells her not	29
to use that word. Scout asks if her father really does defend them and he says he	46
does and tries to explain to Scout the dynamics of race in the small town in which	63
they live.	65
Atticus confides that he is about to defend a black man, Tom Robinson, who	79
is accused of raping a white woman. He does not think he can win the case, but	96
must defend it out of his sense of justice. Atticus tells Scout that things could get	112
difficult for them, but that she must always remember that the people of Maycomb	126
are their friends and that Maycomb is their home. This piece of foreshadowing sets	140
the stage for the events to come and the changes both the Finches and the citizens	156
of Maycomb will endure.	160
When Christmas arrives, so does Uncle Jack, who Scout likes. He gifts the	173
Finch children with much desired air rifles. On Christmas day, Atticus takes Jack,	186
Jem and Scout to Finch Landing where they spend time with Aunt Alexandra and	200
her grandson, Francis. Scout finds Francis boring and as bad as the prissy Aunt	214
Alexandra who makes her dress like a lady, rather then in pants.	226
One evening, Francis calls Atticus a "nigger-lover" and says he is "ruining the	240
family" – words and opinions he's taken from Aunt Alexandra. Scout swears at him	253
and beats him up. Frances tells and Uncle Jack spanks her without even asking	267
about her side – symbolic of the injustice unfolding in the novel.	278
Scout overhears a conversation, that she was quite possibly meant to	289
overhear, between Uncle Jack and her father in which her father expresses his hope	303
that his children can get through the impending case without harnessing the same	316
hatred and prejudice – against people of another race – that most of Maycomb feels.	329
Atticus further tells Jack that he hopes his children will come to him if they have	345
any questions and that Tom Robinson is innocent, but will be convicted nonetheless.	358

Total Words Read:_____
Divided by 2:   _____
Minus errors: _____
= WPM   _____

Comprehension – Chapter 9

Summarize the passage in five sentences: _____

_____

_____

_____

_____

_____

Why does Scout want to fight with Cecil Jacobs?_____

_____

_____

_____

_____

_____

Circle or highlight the correct answer.

1. Who comes for Christmas?
   a) Uncle Jack
   b) Calpurnia
   c) Aunt Alexandra
   d) Tom

2. What is "Finch Landing?"
   a) Where Aunt Alexandra lives
   b) Where Uncle Jack lives
   c) Atticus' home
   d) The town center

3. What did Uncle Jack gift the children?
   a) A fat cat
   b) Air rifles
   c) Popcorn
   d) Clothes

To Kill a Mockingbird – Chapters 10 and 11

Jem and Scout are embarrassed that their father is older than the other dads	14
and that he is rather bookish. One day, however, a mad dog appears and Atticus is	30
asked by the sheriff to shoot the dog. Even though Atticus is pretty far from the	46
animal, he is dead on. The mad dog is symbolic of the injustice and darkness that	62
hovers over race relations in Maycomb, just as Atticus is symbolic of the scales of	77
justice. The children are surprised that their father is such a good shot. He does not	93
hunt and fish like the other fathers. Miss Maudie informs Jem and Scout that	107
Atticus used to be considered the best shot in the county, but they can't tell him she	124
told them because, she reasons, if he wanted them to know he would have told them	140
himself.	141
In second grade now, Scout is more interested in the downtown Maycomb than	154
the mystery of Boo Radley, only to get there she has to pass the house of the rather	172
cranky Mrs. Dubose, who yells at Jem and Scout each time they pass by. At Atticus'	188
prompting, Jem is gentlemanly to the old lady, because she is old and sick. The good	204
behavior lasts until Mrs. Dubose tells the children that their father is trash like the	219
people he works for. Pushed over the edge, Jem destroys Mrs. Dubose's camellia	232
bushes. To make it right, however, Jem has to go to her house and read to her each	250
day for a month. Scout goes with her brother and both children sustain the abuse	265
derived from the woman's fits at the end of each reading session.	277
One evening Mrs. Dubose dies and Atticus tells Jem that the woman was	290
addicted to morphine and that the reading was part of the efforts for her to say	306
sober. Atticus passes along a box, with a single white camellia in it, to Jem. It is a	324
gift from Mrs. Dubose.	328

Total Words Read:_____
Divided by 2:   _____
Minus errors: _____
= WPM   _____

Comprehension – Chapters 10 and 11

Summarize the passage in five sentences: _____

_____

_____

_____

_____

_____

_____

Describe one event from the chapter that is not covered in the passage: _____

_____

_____

_____

_____

_____

_____

How does Scout view her father? _____

_____

_____

_____

_____

_____

_____

What does Atticus do that amazes his children? _____

_____

_____

_____

_____

Circle or highlight the correct answer.

1. Why is Scout a bit ashamed of her father?
   a) He is older and can't do anything
   b) He defends the wrong people
   c) He won't play football
   d) He kills mockingbirds

2. What does Miss Maudie say mockingbirds do?
   a) Eat bird seed
   b) Fly over town
   c) Make a lot of noise
   d) Sing for all to enjoy.

3. What happens to the dog?
   a) It runs away
   b) It gets shot
   c) It bites Jem
   d) It bites Dill

4. Why does Atticus have to leave?
   a) To go on vacation
   b) To defend someone
   c) To capture dogs
   d) To go to the legislative session

5. Why does Jem lose his temper?
   a) Mrs. Dubose tells him that his father is not better than the trash he works for
   b) Mrs. Dubose shoots his dog
   c) Atticus shoots his bog
   d) He doesn't

6. What is in the box that Mrs. Dubose leaves for Jem?
   a) A pink camellia
   b) A white camellia
   c) A rose
   d) A mockingbird

7. The book Jem carried to read to Mrs. Dubose was:
   a) Ivanhoe
   b) King Arthur Returns
   c) To Kill a Mockingbird
   d) The Scarlet Letter

8. Write a two sentence summary of Chapters 10 and 11.

Part I: Activities

Name: _____ Date: _____

The Character and Theme Link (CCSS RL.2)

Choose four characters, link each to one to a theme of *To Kill a Mockingbird*, and site examples of this link through the character's actions, lack of actions, statements, decisions and/or quotes.

Character	Theme	Example
		Page number _____
		Page number _____
		Page number _____
		Page number _____

Character Analysis – How Scout Sees Herself / How Others See Scout (CCSS RL.3)

How Others Sees Scout

How do you see the Scout?

How Scout Sees Herself

Impact of Author's Choice's CCSS RL.3

Choose two characters from *To Kill a Mockingbird* and write their names and main character traits in the arrows. In the middle box, tell how specific events related to each individual, develop and join the characters over the course of the novel.

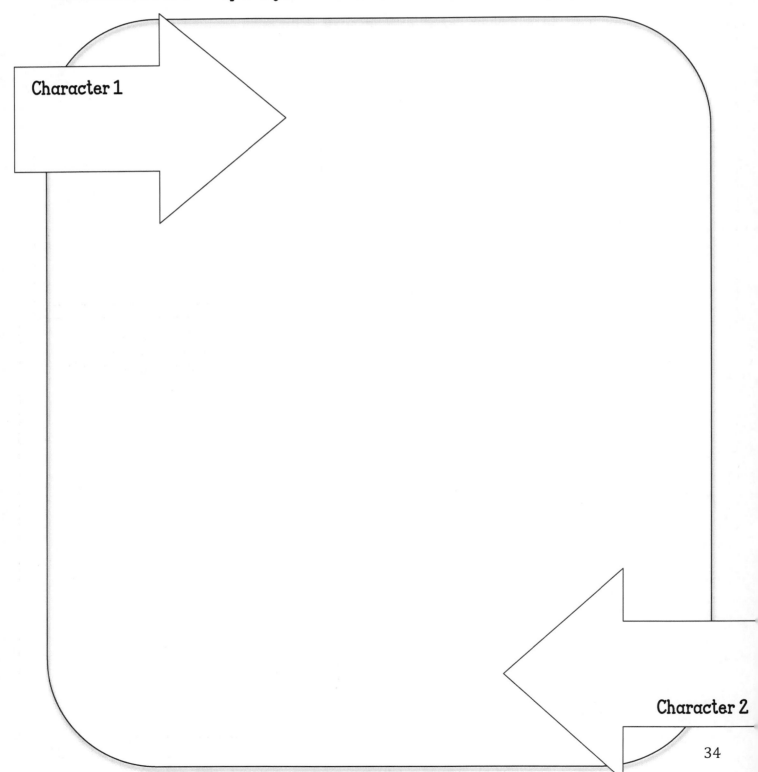

Character 1

Character 2

Name: _____ **Date:** _____

Plot Development – CCSS RL3 – Scout's Contributions

Main Event 2
Discuss how the character's action contribute to the advancement of the plot:

Main Event 3
Discuss how the character's action contribute to the advancement of the plot:

Main Event 1
Discuss how the character's action contribute to the development of the plot:

Main Event 4
Discuss how the character's action contribute to the resolution of the plot:

Start

Plot Development – CCSS RL3 – Boo's Contributions

Main Event 2
Discuss how the character's action contribute to the advancement of the plot:

Main Event 3
Discuss how the character's action contribute to the advancement of the plot:

Main Event 1
Discuss how the character's action contribute to the development of the plot:

Main Event 4
Discuss how the character's action contribute to the resolution of the plot:

Start

Plot Development – CCSS RL3 – The Setting's Contributions

Main Event 2
Discuss how the setting contributes to the advancement of the plot:

Main Event 3
Discuss how the setting contributes to the advancement of the plot:

Main Event 1
Discuss how the setting contributes to the development of the plot:

Main Event 4
Discuss how the setting contributes to the resolution of the plot:

Start

Elements of Part 1: *To Kill a Mockingbird* CCSS RL.3

	How Jem is Shaped by the Story	How the Plot is Shaped by the Story
Setting		
Order Of Events		
Point Of View		
Rising Action		
Conflict		

Name: _____ Date: _____

Dialogue Dissection - CCSS RL.3

Choose quotes from TKAM that propel the action, reveal aspects of a character and provoke a decision.

Propels the action of the novel	Quote:	Page #
	How does it propel the action	
Reveals aspects of a character	Quote:	Page #
	What does the quote reveal about _____?	
Provokes a decision	Quote:	Page #
	What decision is provoked?	

Name: _____ Date: _____

Word Choices – Connotative Meanings -- CCSS RL.4

Connotation refers to a meaning implied by a word apart from its literal meaning. Words carry cultural and emotional associations or meanings in addition to their literal meanings. In the spaces below, analyze the author's word choices.

Examples of Connotative Meanings in *To Kill a Mockingbird*	
Passage or quote from TKAM	
Literal meaning	
Connotative meaning – what emotion does it evoke?	
How does the passage or quote help to set the tone	
How does the passage or quote influence the overall meaning of the section	

Examples of Connotative Meanings in *To Kill a Mockingbird*	
Passage or quote from TKAM	
Literal meaning	
Connotative meaning – what emotion does it evoke?	
How does the passage or quote help to set the tone	
How does the passage or quote influence the overall meaning of the section	

Part II: To Kill a Mockingbird

To Kill a Mockingbird – Chapters 12 and 13

Jem is now twelve and has grown tired of his sister pestering him. He wants her	16
to be more like a girl, which of course upsets her. She is looking forward to summer	33
and the arrival of Dill, only he doesn't come, but rather sends a letter explaining how	49
he has a new father who wants him to stay with his family.	62
To compound this, Atticus is a member of the legislature, which is now in	76
session, and must travel to the state capital every day. Calpurnia takes the children	90
to her "colored" church. The church is in an old building called "First Purchase" –	104
named because it was purchased from the first earnings of freed slaves. The	117
congregation is nice to the children and the reverend welcoming; however, a woman	130
named Lula is critical. The children see how poor the church is.	142
During the service, a collection is taken for Tom Robinson's wife Helen and	155
Scout learns that the man their father is defending is accused by Bob Ewell. Scout	170
can't understand why anyone would believe anything Bob or any other Ewell says.	183
Scout and Jem contribute the money their father gave them to the collection. Scout	197
is shocked that Calpurnia has a life outside of being their cook.	209
Upon returning home, the children find Aunt Alexandra waiting – who explains	220
that she will be staying with them so the children have a feminine influence.	234
Maycomb welcomes her with open arms – ladies of the town bake her cakes, have	248
her over for coffee and soon she is the hub of the small town's social life. Alexandra	265
is proud of the Finch name and spends a good deal of time discussing the families of	282
Maycomb. The Finches are one of the "old" families of the town and there is a pride	299
in the families who have lived there for generations. Their aunt does not like that	314
Jem and Scout lack this pride, but when she encourages Atticus to explain about	328
their ancestry and instill such pride into the children, the only thing it does is makes	344
Scout cry.	346
There are scandals in the Finch family and many of the townspeople are	359
obsessed with the Finch shame. This obsession upsets Aunt Alexandra.	369

Total Words Read:_____
Divided by 2: _____
Minus errors: _____
= WPM _____

Comprehension – Chapter 12 and 13

Summarize the passage in five sentences: _____

_____

_____

_____

_____

_____

Describe one event from the chapter that is not covered in the passage: _____

_____

_____

_____

_____

_____

_____

_____

Describe what the "alien set of values" Jem tries to "impose" Scout in Chapter 12.

_____

_____

_____

_____

_____

_____

Why does Aunt Alexandra come to the Finch household?

_____

_____

_____

_____

_____

Circle or highlight the correct answer.

1. How old is Jem when Chapter 12 opens?
   a) 12- years-old
   b) 8-years-old
   c) 11-years-old
   d) 18-years-old

2. Where did Calpurnia sleep when she stayed overnight at the Finch House?
   a) In Scout's room
   b) On a cot in Scout's room
   c) On a cot in the kitchen
   d) On a cot in the living room

3. What surprises Scout about Calpurnia when they go to church?
   a) That Calpurnia doesn't believe in God
   b) That the church is small
   c) That Calpurnia speaks differently than she does at their home

4. The name of the building that house Calpurnia's church was:
   a) The New Church
   b) Second Purchase
   c) First Purchase
   d) The Old Purchase

5. According to Scout, how long is "for a while" in Maycomb time?
   a) Three months
   b) Three years
   c) One to five years
   d) Three to thirty years

6. What did Aunt Alexandra have a preoccupation with?
   a) Manners
   b) Heredity
   c) The Finch family
   d) Tea

7. How does Atticus tell Jem and Scout they should behave?
   a) Like the lady and gentleman they are
   b) With manners
   c) How he behaves
   d) Better than they are

8. Using complete sentences, please describe the caste system in Maycomb.

To Kill a Mockingbird – Chapter 14 and 15

As Tom Robinson's day in court approaches, the Finch children become objects	12
of whispered comments and backwards glances. Scout overhears someone talking	22
about rape and asks her father what it is. Atticus states it is "carnal knowledge of a	39
female by force without consent." This does not help Scout understand. Scout	51
presses, and can't understand why Calpurnia won't explain it to her. Scout	63
overhears her father and Aunt Alexandra talking. Aunt Alexandra wants to fire	75
Calpurnia, but Atticus will not.	80
Jem urges Scout to quite antagonizing Aunt Alexandra. Scout gets mad and goes	93
after her brother. Atticus sends them to bed – at which time Scout discovers Dill	107
hiding in her room – under her bed. Dill is a nice respite to Aunt Alexandra's adult	123
world and allows Scout to sink back into her childhood, if only for a short time.	139
Dill has run away from home because his mother and new father don't pay any	154
attention to him. He has had an arduous journey and he is hungry. Jem tells his	170
father about Dill. Atticus tells Scout to get him food and then he goes to tell Miss	187
Rachel, his aunt, that Dill is safe and with them. Dill gets into bed with Scout and	204
they talk about their families. His doesn't pay enough attention and hers pays way	218
too much. Dill ends up staying the summer in Maycomb.	220
The town's sheriff, Heck Tate leads some men to the Finch home. Atticus speaks	228
with them on the porch. They are afraid that a lynch mob is gathering for when Tom	242
Robinson will be moved to the Maycomb jail.	259
The next evening, Atticus goes into town. Jem, Scout and Dill follow him. Atticus	267
stands by the jail, four cars drive up and park nearby. They tell Atticus to move. He	281
won't. Scout comes out of her hiding place and sees the men. Jem and Dill come out	298
too. Atticus tells Jem to go home, but he refuses. One of the men tells Atticus that	315
he has fifteen seconds to get his children to leave. Scout realizes that she knows the	332
men. He is the father of her schoolmate, Walter Cunningham. Scout tells him to tell	348
his son "Hey" – a small bit of southern hospitality. All of the men just look at her.	363
This act of innocence, this naivety, shames Mr. Cunningham. He bends to Scout and	380
tells her he will tell Walter hello. Mr. Cunningham tells his counterparts to leave.	394
They all do. She has inadvertently defused the situation by just being kind and	408
sincere.	422
Note: Some have criticized that Scout's easy disbursement of the drunken mob	423
is too easy – that the childhood innocence and southern manners are over played;	435
however, in the world of this novel, the characters make sense and this action	448
makes sense. It is essential for the reader to know that Scout's goodness remains	462
untarnished and her belief in humanity remains whole. This scene also casts a	476
contradictory shadow on the mob – as their own humanity is able to emerge. They	489
are racist, but they are human.	503
	509

Total Words Read:_____ Divided by 2: _____ Minus errors: _____ = WPM _____

Comprehension – Chapters 14 and 15

Summarize the passage in five sentences: _____

_____

_____

_____

_____

_____

Describe one event from the chapter that is not covered in the passage: _____

_____

_____

_____

_____

_____

_____

Describe Scout's relationship with Dill in Chapters 14 and 15. _____

_____

_____

_____

_____

_____

_____

Recount the incident between Scout and Mr. Cunningham. _____

_____

_____

_____

_____

_____

_____

Circle or highlight the correct answer.

1. Scout asked to go to Calpurnia's house. Who said she could not?
   a) Atticus
   b) Calpurnia
   c) Aunt Alexandra
   d) Mr. Finch

2. What did Aunt Alexandra want Atticus to do with Calpurnia?
   a) Give her a raise
   b) Fire her
   c) Move her in
   d) Stop her from going to church

3. Who was found under Jem's bed?
   a) Francis
   b) Scout
   c) Dill
   d) Jem

4. Where does Aunt Alexandra say "babies come from?"
   a) The stork
   b) You kiss and hug good night
   c) God drops them down the chimney
   d) They are left in their cribs by angels

5. What is Atticus' reaction when Jem asked if the group at the door was a gang?
   a) Atticus was concerned
   b) He tried to stifle a smile
   c) He got angry
   d) He turned on the light

6. What does Scout describe as her father's "peculiarities"?
   a) Walking and never eating desserts
   b) Never eating desserts and throwing the football around
   c) Walking and throwing the football around
   d) Walking and eating pie

7. Why does Scout kick "the man"?
   a) He roughly pushed Jem
   b) He roughly pushed her
   c) He roughly tugged on her collar
   d) He roughly tugged on Scout's collar

8. How does Scout defuse the incident outside of the courthouse?

To Kill a Mockingbird – Chapter 16 and 17

When the trial begins people, from all over the county, descend upon the small town	15
of Maycomb. Miss Maudie seems to be the only person who refuses to go to the trial. The	68
children are in the courthouse and notice all of the different people. At lunchtime, they	83
eat in the square with all of the people there for the trial – some they know and others	101
they do not. Among the spectators is the symbolic Mr. Raymond, who is white but who	117
sits with the black people.	122
Jem informs his sister and Dill that Mr. Raymond has children by a black woman.	137
Mr. Raymond is from an old family and he was once engaged to a white women, only she	155
shot herself right before their wedding – perhaps because she discovered her fiancé had	168
a black mistress. Jem explains that he is a drunk but treats his mixed-race children	184
well. Scout asks what a mixed child is and Jem says they are biracial and sad because	202
they don't belong to either side of the very real and very austere racial divide that	218
plagues Maycomb.	220
It stands out that Scout notices that one can't tell that Mr. Raymond's children are	235
not black, so she wonders how they know that they, the Finches, are all white. Jem	251
recounts that their Uncle Jack says one can't know for sure what happened a long time	267
ago, but once one has "a drop of Negro blood, that makes you all black."	282
Lunch ends and everyone lines up to go back inside – the white people in the front	298
and the black people in the back. Scout gets separated from Dill and Jem and overhears	314
that her father was appointed to represent Tom Robinson. She is reunited with her	328
friend and brother, but there aren't any seats left in the white section. The reverend from	344
Calpurnia's church takes the children up to the balcony and the four sit in the front row.	361
They watch the prosecutor question the sheriff, Heck Tate, who recounts that, on	371
the night of November 21, Bob Ewell told him that his daughter Mayella had been raped.	386
When the sheriff arrived at the Ewell home, he found Mayella beaten. She has bruises on	402
the left side of her face. She told him that Tom Robinson had raped her.	417
Bob Ewell is next to take the stand. Bob and his family live behind the town garbage	434
dump. No one knows how many children he has. The house is a cabin and the yard is	462
full of trash; however in one corner there are beautiful and cared for flowers that belong	478
to Mayella. Ewell is a gruff, rude little man. He testifies that when he was coming out of	496
the woods with some kindling he heard his daughter yelling. When he got to the house,	512
he looked in a window and saw Tom Robinson raping his daughter. Robinson fled, Ewell	527
went into the house to make sure his daughter was okay and then he went for the	544
sheriff.	545
On cross-examination, Atticus asks why he did not call a doctor. Ewell said it was	561
too expensive. Atticus has Ewell write his name and the jury sees he is left-handed and	578
thus he would be more likely to leave bruises on the right side if Mayella's face. This	595
excites Jem. Scout is not convinced as Tom Robinson may be left-handed as well and	611
besides, he looks strong enough to beat up Mayella.	620

Total Words Read:_____   Divided by 2: _____   Minus errors: _____ = WPM _____

Comprehension – Chapter 16 and 17

Summarize the passage in five sentences: _____

_____

_____

_____

_____

_____

Describe one event from the chapter that is not covered in the passage: _____

_____

_____

_____

_____

_____

_____

_____

What does Reverend Sykes do for Jem and Scout in Chapter 16? _____

_____

_____

_____

_____

_____

_____

Describe where Bob Ewell lives. _____

_____

_____

_____

_____

_____

_____

Circle or highlight the correct answer.

1. About whom is Scout speaking when she says "I thought _____ was our friend?
   a) Atticus
   b) Calpurnia
   c) Mr. Cunningham
   d) Mr. Finch

2. How did the children gauge Miss Maude's mood?
   a) By her facial features
   b) By her voice
   c) By the way she spoke
   d) By the way she stood

3. What does Jem say is in Mr. Dolphus Raymond's Coca-Cola bottle?
   a) Coca-Cola
   b) Sprite
   c) Water
   d) Whiskey

4. According to Jem, what is a mixed child?
   a) "Half white, half colored"
   b) "Have white, half Cunningham"
   c) "one who hasn't been to school
   d) "One parent from Alabama, one not"

5. What question does Atticus ask three times?
   a) "Did you call a doctor, Sheriff?"
   b) "Did you pull out your badge, Sheriff?"
   c) "What time did you arrive?"
   d) "Did you know Ewell before the call?"

6. The name of the accused is?
   a) Tim Robinson
   b) Tom Robinson
   c) Bob Ewell
   d) Mr. Cunningham

7. Why does Atticus pull out paper and a fountain pen?
   a) To get a writing sample to determine which hand Ewell writes with
   b) To get a writing sample to determine which hand Cunningham writes with
   c) To take down notes
   d) To write a list

8. Describe why it matters that Mr. Ewell is left-handed.

Name: _____ **Date:** _____ **#** _____

To Kill a Mockingbird – **Chapter 18 and 19**

Nineteen-year-old Mayella Ewell testifies next. She is frightened and the reader	13
learns that she has seven siblings who do not help out and can't read or write. She	30
also has a father who is a drunk and no friends. When asked why she did not fight	48
harder and why her screams didn't alert the other children and how Tom Robinson	62
could have bruised the right side of her face when his left hand was useless because	78
it was torn by a cotton gin accident – she doesn't have a real answer.	92
Atticus asks the girl to admit that there was no rape and that her father beat	108
her. She throws a fit and refuses to answer any more questions. She ends by saying	124
"That nigger yonder took advantage of me an' if you fine fancy gentlemen don't wanta	139
do nothin' about it then you're all yellow stinkin' cowards."	149
After a break, the judge asks Atticus if he will be able to finish his case by	166
tomorrow. Atticus responds, with only one witness left to call, that he certainly can.	170
Tom Robinson is the last witness Atticus calls. Tom testifies that Mayella asks	183
him to do chores for her occasionally and that on November 21, the evening in	198
question, she asked him to come and fix a door. He went inside and nothing was	214
wrong with the door and all of her brothers and sisters were gone. He stated that	230
Mayella came on to him and then her father arrived and called her a whore and	246
threatened to kill him. Tom fled.	252
At this point, Tom Robinson's white employer jumps up and says that in eight	266
years Tom has never been trouble. The judge bans the employer from the courtroom	280
for interrupting.	282
The prosecutor cross-examines Tom and points out that Tom is strong enough to	296
chop up furniture with his one good hand and insists that running is a definite sign	312
of guilt. Tom claims he ran because he knew white people would assume he was	327
guilty no matter what.	331
Dill is upset by the whole thing and can't stop crying. Jem makes Scout take	346
him out of the courtroom. Dill tells Scout that he hated to see how the prosecutor	363
spoke to Tom. This highlight's Dill's childish innocence. He responds to the evilness	376
with tears and to the prejudice with disgust.	384

Total Words Read:_____
Divided by 2:   _____
Minus errors: _____
= WPM   _____

Comprehension – Chapter 18 and 19

Summarize the passage in five sentences: _____

_____

_____

_____

_____

_____

Describe one event from the chapter that is not covered in the passage: _____

_____

_____

_____

_____

_____

_____

Describe way "Mayella was raging". _____

_____

_____

_____

_____

_____

_____

What is the matter with Tom Robinson's hand and why may it be significant? _____

_____

_____

_____

_____

_____

_____

Circle or highlight the correct answer.

1. Who is the accuser in the trial?
   a) Atticus
   b) Bob Ewell
   c) Mayelle Ewell
   d) Mr. Finch

2. How long does Mayella say that she had been in school?
   a) 8 years
   b) 10 or 11 years
   c) 11 or 12 years
   d) 2 or 3 years

3. When does Mayella say her father is not "tollable" or tolerable"
   a) When he is riled
   b) When he has been drinking
   c) When he beats her
   d) She retracts her statement

4. What does Jem say when Scout points out that Mr. Underwook saw them?
   a) He'll tell Atticus
   b) He'll put it on the social side of the Tribune
   c) He'll tell Aunt Alexandra
   d) Nothing

5. Why does Tom Robinson pass the Ewell house every day?
   a) Because it is on his way to and from work
   b) Because it is on his way to the store
   c) Because he likes to walk that way
   d) He doesn't say anything

6. Tom Robinson said he ran because:
   a) He was scared
   b) He liked to run
   c) Mr. Ewell was shooting at him
   d) He was late

7. Who stood up in the trial and spoke on behalf of Tom Robinson?
   a) His employer Link Deas
   b) His friend Link Deas
   c) His mother and father
   d) Scout Finch

8. Why did Jem make Scout leave the courtroom?

To Kill a Mockingbird – **Chapter 20 and 21**

Mr. Raymond sympathizes with Dill and offers him a drink from a paper sack.	14
Dill drinks some of the liquid. Scout warns him not to drink too much of it. Dill	31
informs her that it's only Coke. Mr. Raymond admits to Dill and Scout that he only	47
pretends to drink to give the white townspeople an excuse for his lifestyle – but that	62
he really just likes black people better than white people and isn't a drunk at all.	78
Scout and Dill return to the courtroom to see Atticus' closing. He reexamines the	92
evidence and tries to appeal to the jury. Atticus highlights that the prosecution has	106
no medical evidence a crime was even committed, that witness testimony is not	119
reliable and that the bruises suggest Mayella's father, rather than Tom Robinson,	131
bruised her face. Atticus appeals to the jury to cast aside prejudice and the	143
assumption that black people are criminals by nature.	151
As Atticus finishes, Calpurnia enters the courtroom and hands him a note from	164
Aunt Alexandra that says the children are missing. They beg to stay and are allowed	179
to come back to hear the verdict after they have their dinner. Aunt Alexandra is not	195
happy when she hears where they've been and is mortified when she learns they	209
have permission to return.	213
The children return. The jury is still out and everyone is still there. Jem thinks	228
Atticus has won his case. The Reverend tells him that black people don't win over	243
white people.	245
At the end of the chapter, night has fallen and the jury finally returns. Scout	260
notices that they do not look at Tom Robinson. The verdict is guilty. When Atticus	275
leaves, the people sitting in the balcony stand as a sign of respect for him and the	282
work he's done.	285

Total Words Read: _____
Divided by 2:   _____
Minus errors: _____
= WPM   _____

Name: _____ **Date:** _____ **#** _____

Comprehension – Chapter 20 and 21

Summarize the passage in five sentences: _____

_____

_____

_____

_____

_____

Describe one event from the chapter that is not covered in the passage: _____

_____

_____

_____

_____

_____

_____

_____

What happens when Dill drinks from Mr. Raymond's sack? _____

_____

_____

_____

_____

_____

_____

What does the note to Atticus say? _____

_____

_____

_____

_____

_____

_____

Circle or highlight the correct answer.

1. What is the drink Mr. Raymond offers Dill?
   a) Whiskey
   b) water
   c) Coca-Cola
   d) Root beer

2. In Chapter 20, Atticus does something Scout had never seen before:
   a) He unbuttoned his vest in public and loosened his tie and collar
   b) He took a drink of water
   c) Wore a hat
   d) Took off his hat

3. Who entered the courtroom and walked straight up to Atticus?
   a) Jem and Scout Finch
   b) Calpurnia
   c) Aunt Alexandra
   d) Uncle Jack

4. When Jem and Scout were called downstairs from the balcony, Atticus looked:
   a) Angry
   b) Mad
   c) Peeved
   d) Exhausted

5. How did Aunt Alexandra react when Calpurnia told her where they'd been?
   a) Almost fainted
   b) Sent them to their rooms
   c) Laughed
   d) Yelled at them

True or False

_____ Dill fell asleep on Jem's shoulder waiting for the verdict

_____ Aunt Alexandra was happy the children were able to experience the trial

_____ Tom Robinson was found not guilty

_____ Tom Robinson picked cotton

_____ Jem, Scout and Dill sat in the balcony in the section for black people

_____ Calpurnia was angry the children were watching Atticus

_____ Jem and Scout call their father Atticus

_____ Atticus claimed that Mayella "tempted a negro"

56

To Kill a Mockingbird – Chapter 22 and 23

Jem is taken at the injustice of it all and cries. Even Aunt Alexandra tells Atticus	16
that she is sorry he lost the case, but wishes the children had not been allowed to be	34
there. Atticus counters that they have to deal with racism.	44
As the Finches enjoy a breakfast feast from the gifts of food brought by what	59
seems like every black family in Maycomb, Atticus tells his family that there will be	74
an appeal	76
Later, Miss Stephanie Crawford is visiting with Mr. Avery and Miss Maudie, she	89
questions Jem and Scout about the trial. Miss Maudie saves the children by inviting	103
them for cake. Jem explains that his view of Maycomb is altered. He thought that	117
the people in his small town were the best and mostly harbored the same values as	133
he did. The trial has changed all that.	141
Miss Maudie tells him that there are people who tried to help – like Judge Taylor,	156
who assigned their father to Tom Robinson rather than assigning the public	168
defender. She points out that the jury staying out so long must indicate that there is	184
at least some positive movement in the area of race relations.	195
The children leave Miss Maudie's – only to discover – from Miss Stephanie – that	207
Bob Ewell has attacked their father, spitting on him and declaring revenge. The	220
children are nervous that Bob Ewell will hurt their father.	230
Tom Robinson is sent seventy miles away, too far for his family to visit him.	245
Atticus tells his children that the appeal will take some time, but he feels there is a	263
good chance Tom Robinson will be pardoned. Scout asks what happens if he is not	278
and discovers that rape is a capital offense in Alabama. Jem and Atticus discuss the	293
justice of execution for rape and how all twelve men on the jury voted to convict. The	310
theme of prejudice swells as Atticus informs his son that they were lucky to have the	325
jury out so long and that one man, a Cunningham no less, wanted to acquit.	340
Scout is pleased with this and wants to have Walter Cunningham over for	353
dinner, but Aunt Alexandra will not allow "white trash" to associate with them.	376
Scout is angry. She and Jem talk about how their aunt looks down on the	391
Cunninghams and the Cunninghams on the Ewells and everyone down on black	403
people. They are unable to determine why people go out of their way not to like	420
others – this brings the conversation back to Boo Radley – and they wonder if	433
perhaps he doesn't leave the house to stay away from all of the contradiction and	448
craziness of the real world.	453

Total Words Read:_____
Divided by 2:   _____
Minus errors: _____
= WPM   _____

Comprehension – Chapter 22 and 23

Summarize the passage in five sentences: _____

_____

_____

_____

_____

_____

Describe one event from the chapter that is not covered in the passage: _____

_____

_____

_____

_____

_____

_____

As the chapter opens, Jem is crying. Why? _____

_____

_____

_____

_____

_____

_____

Why wasn't Atticus worried about Mr. Bob Ewell's threats? _____

_____

_____

_____

_____

_____

_____

Circle or highlight the correct answer.

1. Who sent over food for the Finch family?
   a) The white community
   b) Calpurnia
   c) The black community
   d) Mr. Finch

2. Miss Stephanie Crawford was visiting:
   a) Only Miss Maudie
   b) Only Mr. Avery
   c) The Finches
   d) Miss Maudie and Mr. Avery

3. Atticus tells them who almost hung the jury?
   a) Mr. Deas
   b) Miss Maudie
   c) A Finch
   d) A Cunningham

4. Jem says the Cunninghams are "yappy". What does he mean?
   a) They talk a lot
   b) They don't bathe enough
   c) They're tacky
   d) They're smart

5. Why does Aunt Alexandra ultimately tell Scout she can't play with Walter.
   a) He's dirty
   b) He is a Cunningham
   c) He's trash
   d) He's too old

6. What kind of candy does Scout present to Jem and say "have a chew?"
   a) Taffy
   b) A Tootsie Roll
   c) A Lifesaver
   d) Fudge

7. How does Jem describe background to Scout.
   a) Being from an old family
   b) How long your family has been able to read or write
   c) How long your family has lived in Maycomb
   d) How long he has known someone

8. What does Jem say of Boo Radley at the end of Chapter 23?
   a) He wants to meet him
   b) Boo is crazy
   c) Boo stayed shut in his house because he wanted to
   d) That they need to stop bugging Boo

To Kill a Mockingbird – **Chapters 24 and 25**

One day Aunt Alexandra invites her missionary circle group to tea. Scout,	12
dressed like a lady, helps Calpurnia bring in the tea. Her aunt is so pleased with her	29
that she asks her to stay. Scout listens as the ladies discuss a poor African tribe,	46
the Mrunas, who are being converted to Christianity. The conversation drifts to their	59
own black servants who've been behaving badly after Tom Robinson's trial. One lady,	72
Mrs. Merriweather, even suggests that it is important for these gossiping women to	85
remind their servants that Jesus was never cranky about anything so they should	98
strive to be the same. Note the irony here.	107
Miss Maudie quashes their chatter with biting comments. Atticus appears and	118
calls Alexandra into the kitchen. He tells Scout, Alexandra and Miss Maudie that	131
Tom Robinson tried to escape and was shot seventeen times. Atticus takes	143
Calpurnia with him to the Robinson's house to tell them about his death.	156
Alexandra wonders to Miss Maudie how Atticus can ruin himself over a pursuit	169
of justice. Maudie tells her that the town trusts Atticus to do what is right.	184
September returns and it is a hot one. Jem and Scout are sleeping on the porch.	200
Scout is playing with a roly poly bug. Jem stops his sister just as she is about to	218
squish it. Scout makes fun of him and thinks he's the one who is turning into a girl.	236
Dill has gone home again, but Scout is thinking about him and how he told her	252
that Jem and he ran into Atticus as he and Calpurnia were going to the Robinson's	268
house to tell Helen that Tom Robinson had been shot and was dead.	281
There is a buzz over Maycomb regarding Tom Robinson's death. Mr. Underwood	293
writes about how the death is the murder of an innocent man. Bob Ewell comments	308
that Tom's death is "one down and two more to go."	319

Total Words Read:_____
Divided by 2:   _____
Minus errors: _____
= WPM   _____

Comprehension – Chapter 24 and 25

Summarize the passage in five sentences: _____

_____

_____

_____

_____

_____

Describe one event from the chapter that is not covered in the passage: _____

_____

_____

_____

_____

_____

_____

Describe Aunt Alexandra's tea. _____

_____

_____

_____

_____

_____

_____

What does Atticus tell Jem to do regarding Bob Ewell? _____

_____

_____

_____

_____

_____

_____

Circle or highlight the correct answer.

1. What did Jem tell Scout not to mash?
   a) A kitten
   b) A cat
   c) A roly poly
   d) A lightening bug

2. How does Dill tell Scout Helen Robinson reacts to the news Tom Robinson was shot?
   a) She cries
   b) She falls down in the dirt
   c) She sobs
   d) She moves to a different town.

3. What does Scout do that pleases Aunt Alexandra?
   a) Scout acts and dresses like a lady
   b) Scout serves tea
   c) Scout stays quite for a change
   d) Scout reads to her

4. Why does Atticus call Aunt Alexandra into the kitchen?
   a) To tell her he is going out
   b) To tell her he shot a dog
   c) To tell her Tom Robinson had been shot
   d) To ask her for some tea

5. Who says "one down and one to go?"
   a) Ewell
   b) Finch
   c) Cunningham
   d) Jem

6. There was a brief obituary for Tom Robinson in which paper?
   a) The Maycomb Explorer
   b) The Maycomb Tribune
   c) The Maycomb Chronicle
   d) The Alabama Review

7. Who did Atticus ask to accompany him to speak with Helen Robinson?
   a) The Sheriff
   b) The newspaper man
   c) Calpurnia
   d) Aunt Alexandra

8. Where does Atticus tell Jem and Dill they have to stay if they come with him?
   a) In the front yard
   b) In the car
   c) In the backseat

To Kill a Mockingbird – Chapters 26 and 27

School begins again, as does the daily passing of Boo Radley's house. Scout and	14
Jem are no longer afraid of the house or Boo – symbolic of the transition they are	30
making from childhood and the overall theme of maturity and childhood lost. Scout	43
just wishes she could see Boo for herself.	51
Jem and Scout try to act like a lady and a gentleman at school – as most of the	69
children the deal with are mirrors of their parents' prejudices. Scout is confused and	83
wonders why, if everyone disagrees with her father and his moral code, they	96
continue to elect him to represent them in the legislature?	106
In school, Miss Gates, Scout's teacher, ironically talks about the persecution of	118
the Jews and the importance, and even moral virtue, of equality. Scout takes it all	133
in, remembering that when Miss Gates came out of the trial she commented that it	148
was about time someone taught the blacks in their town a lesson. Scout asks Jem	163
about it and he gets angry and tells her never, ever to talk to him about the trial	181
again. Scout goes to her father for comfort. She sits on his lap, but doesn't exactly fit	198
anymore – again symbolic of her continual grown.	205
Bob Ewell gets a job in one of the Depression work programs only to lose it a few	223
days later. He blames Atticus for this. About the same time, Judge Taylor is home	238
alone and hears something. When he investigates, he notices his screen door is open	252
and he sees a shadow slinking away. Atticus and Judge Taylor are the "two to go" or	269
so it seems.	272
Bob Ewell has also taken to following Helen Robinson to work, whispering	284
obscenities at her. Deas, Tom Robinson's employer who spoke up for him at the	298
trial, tells Ewell he'll have him arrested if he continues harassing Helen. Bob stops,	312
only Aunt Alexandra is worried as Bob is unstable and seems to harbor a grudge	327
against anyone connected to the case.	333
On Halloween, the town hosts a school pageant. It is an agriculture themed	346
event and Scout is dressed up like a ham. Jem takes her to the school because	362
Atticus and Aunt Alexander are too exhausted to go.	371

Total Words Read:_____
Divided by 2:   _____
Minus errors: _____
= WPM   _____

Comprehension – Chapter 26 and 27

Summarize the passage in five sentences: _____

_____

_____

_____

_____

_____

Describe one event from the chapter that is not covered in the passage: _____

_____

_____

_____

_____

_____

_____

Tell how Scout feels about the Radley Place at the beginning of Chapter 26? _____

_____

_____

_____

_____

_____

_____

How does Bob Ewell harass Helen Robinson? _____

_____

_____

_____

_____

_____

_____

Circle or highlight the correct answer.

1. How does Scout describe the events of the summer?
   a) They were exciting
   b) The hung over them like a damp cloth
   c) They hung over them like smoke in a closed room
   d) They were finally over

2. Who did Cecil Jacobs talk about for his current event?
   a) FDR
   b) Adolf Hitler
   c) Scout Finch
   d) Dill's aunt Miss Rachel

3. Miss Gates is:
   a) Scout's new neighbor
   b) Scout's aunt's friend
   c) Scout's teacher
   d) Jem's teacher

4. How much weight does Jem have to gain to in order to play ball?
   a) Ten pounds
   b) Twenty pounds
   c) Twenty-five pounds
   d) Thirty pounds

5. Who stood up for Helen Robinson when Mr. Ewell was harassing her?
   a) Mr. Link
   b) Calpurnia
   c) Jem
   d) Scout

6. What did Cecil Jacob ask Scout?
   a) If she would play with him
   b) If he could come over for supper
   c) If Atticus was a Radical
   d) If she knew about Adolf Hitler

7. What was happening this October in the high school auditorium?
   a) A Halloween festival
   b) A ball game
   c) Miss Tutti and Miss Frutti's concert
   d) Nothing

8. Scout's costume was:
   a) A piggy
   b) A cat
   c) A cured ham
   d) A chicken thigh

To Kill a Mockingbird – Chapters 28 through 31

The evening is already dark and as they are walking to school Cecil Jacobs	14
jumps out and frightens Scout and Jem and then tags along. Scout and her friend	29
visit the haunted house in the seventh grade classroom and buy homemade candy.	42
Then the children go backstage for the pageant. Scout misses her entrance because	55
she's fallen asleep – when she runs onstage at the end – the judge and others laugh.	70
Scout is accused of ruining the pageant. Scout feels so bad that she and Jem wait	86
backstage until the people are gone before they leave.	95
They leave school and Scout tells her brother she forgot her shoes, when they go	110
to retrieve them, the lights go off in the school so they decide she will get them later.	128
Jem seems anxious and hushes Scout, telling her he hears something. She tells him	142
she's too old for games such as this – but he tells her he is not playing. At first they	161
brush it off as Cecil again. Scout yells a tease out to Cecil. They get no response.	178
Scout realizes that Jem knows they are not being followed by Cecil and that he	193
is only pretending it is him so she doesn't get frightened. They see someone running	208
towards them – a grown man. Jem yells at Scout to run. She hears fighting, but	223
can't see anything. Scout hears Jem scream. She runs towards the scream and	236
bumps into a man. The man squeezes her until she can no longer breathe, but then	252
he falls. She thinks Jem must have gotten up to help her. Scout calls for Jem, but	269
he doesn't answer. Eventually, she spots a man carrying Jem. He heads to the Finch	284
house where Atticus lets him in and then calls the doctor and the sheriff. Aunt	299
Alexandra questions Scout, but she truly doesn't know what happened. Jem has a	312
concussion and broken arm. The doctor examines Scout as well.	322
The sheriff arrives with the news that he's found a pink dress, some pieces of	337
ham colored cloth and the stabbed, dead body of Bob Ewell.	352
Scout tries to remember what happened and tells everyone what she heard and	365
saw. Sheriff Heck Tate shows them her costume with a slash on it where a knife	381
stabbed at it, but was stopped by the wire. Scout tells them that Jem was picked up	398
and carried and she looks at the man in the corner and realizes it is Boo Radley. He	416
smiles shyly at her and she movingly says, "Hey Boo".	426
Boo and Scout sit on the porch and listen to the sheriff and her father talking.	442
The sheriff is calling Bob Ewell's death an accident, but Atticus thinks Jem killed	456
him. Sheriff Tate tells Atticus that Ewell fell on his own knife. Tate knows that Boo	472
is the one who stabbed Ewell, but doesn't want the poor man to receive the attention	488
or wrath of the neighborhood.	493
Tom Robinson is dead for no reason and so is the man responsible for his death.	514
The sheriff astutely comments: "Let the dead bury the dead." Scout escorts Boo	527
home, after they go and check on her brother. Scout never sees Boo again, but is	543
now able to see the world from his perspective. Atticus is in Jem's room and her	559
father reads to her until she falls asleep.	567

Total Words Read:_____ Divided by 2: _____ Minus errors: _____ = WPM _____

Comprehension – Chapters 28 through 30

Summarize the passage in five sentences: _____

_____

_____

_____

_____

_____

Describe one event from the chapter that is not covered in the passage: _____

_____

_____

_____

_____

_____

_____

Why do Jem and Scout need to go back to the high school gym? _____

_____

_____

_____

_____

_____

_____

Who rescues Jem and how does the rescue happen? _____

_____

_____

_____

_____

_____

_____

Circle or highlight the correct answer.

1. Who frightens Jem and Scout on their way to the Halloween event?
   a) Miss Stephanie
   b) Cecil Jacobs
   c) Miss Maudie
   d) Dill

2. Who did they buy homemade divinity from?
   a) Miss Stephanie
   b) Miss Maudie
   c) Calpurnia
   d) Mrs. Taylor

3. Why does Scout miss her cue to go onstage?
   a) She is reading
   b) She is talking
   c) She fell asleep
   d) She forgot what the cue was

4. What happens when Scout calls for Jem?
   a) He calls back
   b) He runs
   c) He doesn't answer
   d) He takes her home

5. Who does Atticus call first?
   a) The doctor
   b) The sheriff
   c) The newspaper
   d) Aunt Alexandra

6. Who carried Jem Finch home?
   a) Arthur Radley
   b) Nathan Radley
   c) Cecil Jacobs
   d) Mr. Ewell

7. What does Scout say to Boo Radley when she finally meets him?
   a) Nice to meet you
   b) Hey Boo
   c) Hi Boo
   d) Hello Boo

8. Who killed Mr. Ewell?
   a) Jem
   b) Scout
   c) Boo
   d) Dill

Part II: Activities

Word Choices – Meaning Over the Span of the Text -- CCSS RL.4

Word: _____

Definition or meaning at the beginning of the text: _____

_____

How the word was used later in the text: _____

_____

How the meaning of the word changed over the span of the text: _____

_____

_____

What affect did the change have on you, the reader? _____

_____

_____

_____

Why does the change in meaning matter to the overall story? _____

_____

_____

_____

Structure – Foreshadowing and Flashbacks -- CCSS RL.5

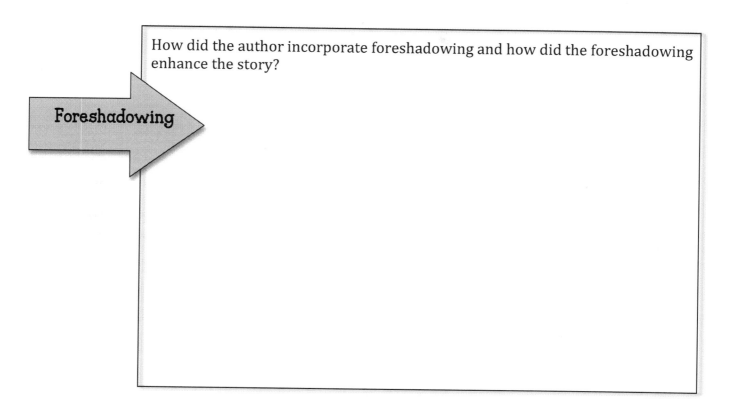

How did the author incorporate foreshadowing and how did the foreshadowing enhance the story?

Foreshadowing

How did the author incorporate flashbacks and how did the flashbacks enhance the story?

Flashbacks

Book vs. Movie

How do the images on the screen compare to your own interpretation of the setting?

_____

_____

How to the events in the movie compare to the events in the novel?

_____

_____

How do the characterizations from the novel compare to the those of the movie?

_____

_____

What are the main differences between the movie and the novel?

_____

_____

_____

_____

Why do you think the changes you listed above were made?

_____

_____

_____

_____

Name: _____ **Date:** _____

Historical vs. Fictional Portrayals in Literature – CCSS RL.9

Directions: Compare the non-fictional passage, at the provided link, to the live and times in *To Kill a Mockingbird.*

Setting: _____ ____

_____

_____

How does TKAM relate to the events from this time period? _____

_____

_____

Why do you think the author choose race relations in the small town in Alabama to fictionalize?

_____

_____

_____

_____

How does this story help to bring the history of the South in the 1930s to life?

_____

_____

_____

_____

Have your views changed about this time period or the surrounding historical events after reading *To Kill a Mockingbird*? Why or why not?

_____

http://www.encyclopediaofalabama.org/article/h-2128

Name: _____ Date: _____ #_____

Alabama and the Great Depression

Read: The Great Depression and Alabama http://www.encyclopediaofalabama.org/article/h-3608 from the Encyclopedia of Alabama.

After World War I, Alabama saw the same economic boom as the rest of America. The war stimulated manufacturing and Alabama's rich and diversified industrial sector featured functioning and relatively prosperous textile mills, coalmines, steel and iron mills and timber mills. The growth in population mirrored the industrial and business growth in the state where labor was both cheap and abundant – until about 1926.

Then there was agriculture, which became depressed over the course of the 1920s – affecting a full 78% of the population of Alabama – all of which lived in rural areas. So when the Crash of November 1929 hit – Alabama was overwhelmed by the need to provide relief to its poor and downtrodden.

Little was done to help, until Franklin Roosevelt became president in 1933 and relief and reform efforts, under the moniker "the New Deal" were initiated. The New Deal programs were designed to *give a hand up, not a hand out*". Alabama had long struggled with poverty and illiteracy that were generationally ingrained that the efforts of the New Deal did little to add much relief. The demand for greater federal and state assistance continued to increase – as did the need for a complete restructuring of the antiquated economic system embedded in the farm tenancy which had long illustrated the agricultural economy in Alabama.

Site three examples of evidence of the Great Depression from <u>To Kill a Mockingbird</u>. Be sure to include the page number and how you know it is an example.

| |
| |
| |

http://www.archives.alabama.gov/teacher/dep/dep.html

Socratic Discussion/Seminar Instructions

Common Core Anchor Standards Addressed: R1, R2, R5, W1, W9, SL1 and SL4

A Socratic Seminar is a structured discussion that allows students to engage and disagree in a way that is polite, focused and respectful. This activity enables students to think critically about texts and build confidence in their ideas and thought processes.

Students begin Socratic Seminars with a list of teacher (or student, depending upon the level) generated questions that help the group think critically about the text they are reading. Students pose questions to the group and take turns speaking and listening to each other's thoughts and ideas. All members of the discussion share learning as students work together to gain a deeper understanding of the text – as they extend, clarify and challenge themselves and each other.

Hint: Before you begin this activity, develop a signal to politely stop any student who may be dominating the conversation.

Students should complete a Seminar Template so they truly understand the text and their argument. A blank template immediately follows these instructions. This work may be done individually, in groups or as a whole class activity. If students are remedial or need extra help – working as a class, especially through the first few Socratic Discussions/Seminars – is extremely helpful.

1. Break into groups and circle up – or circle up one group with leftover students circled around the discussion group. The outer circle will act as scribes.

2. Establish and/or discuss the rules and norms of the discussion.

3. Review the purpose of the activity and your expectations. Model how students should participate and behave.

4. Select a discussion leader.

5. Set a time limit: 30 to 40 minutes is sufficient.

6. Begin the discussion.

7. Debrief: include discussing the groups strengths and weaknesses.

Helpful Hints: If your class is large, divide students into two circles, one inner and one outer. Leave one chair in the inner circle empty. This is the "roving seat." Students who are in the inner circle are active discussion members. Students in the outer circle can pop in and contribute. If it is not the first time you are doing this activity – you may actually have two seminars going at the same time. Twenty students is about the limit for active participation to be effective for all students; however, students are more engaged if group size is closer to twelve.

It is imperative to stress that students must reference the text often and that thinking and analyzing out of the box are essential – and encouraged – for this activity. Teachers should stay out of the conversation, but guide if necessary.

Name: _____ Date: _____ # _____

To Kill a Mockingbird Socratic Seminar

(empty oval)

Site two main ideas or claims from the novel to support your argument as it relates to the question.

1. _____
   _____
   _____
   _____
   _____ page:

2. _____
   _____
   _____
   _____
   _____ page:

List examples SUPPORTING your argument:

List examples COUNTERING your argument:

To Kill a Mockingbird – **Chapter 1 Socratic Seminar**

Scout says of her mother: "Our mother died when I was two, so I never felt her absence. She was a Graham from Montgomery…" What does the quote imply about being an outsider in Maycomb?

Site two main ideas or claims from the novel to support your argument as it relates to the question.

1. _____
_____
_____
_____
_____ page:

2. _____
_____
_____
_____
_____ page:

List examples SUPPORTING your argument:

List examples COUNTERING your argument:

Name: _____ **Date:** _____ **#** _____

To Kill a Mockingbird –Socratic Seminar

Was the prejudice of the townspeople of Maycomb responsible
for Tom Robinson's death?

Site two main ideas or claims from the novel to support your argument as it relates to the question.

1. _____

_____

_____

_____

_____

_____ page:

2. _____

_____

_____

_____

_____

_____ page:

List examples SUPPORTING your argument:

List examples COUNTERING your argument:

To Kill a Mockingbird –Socratic Seminar

How is innocence lost?
Is it a negative thing?

Site two main ideas or claims from the novel to support your argument as it relates to the question.

1. _____
_____
_____
_____
_____
_____ page:

2. _____
_____
_____
_____
_____
_____ page:

List examples SUPPORTING your argument:

List examples COUNTERING your argument:

To Kill a Mockingbird –Socratic Seminar

Who are the mockingbirds?
How are they symbolic?

Site two main ideas or claims from the novel to support your argument as it relates to the question.

1. _____
_____
_____
_____
_____ page: _____

2. _____
_____
_____
_____
_____ page: _____

List examples SUPPORTING your argument:

List examples COUNTERING your argument:

To Kill a Mockingbird –**Socratic Seminar**

How do race and gender intersect in the novel?

How would the novel be different if it was narrated by Jem? By Calpurnia?

Site two main ideas or claims from the novel to support your argument as it relates to the question.

1. _____
   _____
   _____
   _____
   _____ page:

2. _____
   _____
   _____
   _____
   _____ page:

List examples SUPPORTING your argument:

List examples COUNTERING your argument:

Name: _____ **Date:** _____ # _____

To Kill a Mockingbird –Socratic Seminar

There is an underlying prejudice in the way Atticus Finch lives his life. True or false?

Site two main ideas or claims from the novel to support your argument as it relates to the question.

1. _____
_____
_____
_____
_____ page:

2. _____
_____
_____
_____
_____ page:

List examples SUPPORTING your argument:

List examples COUNTERING your argument:

Socratic Seminar: Participant Rubric

Participant's name: _____ Date: _____

	4	3	2	1
Participant offers solid analysis, without prompting, to move the conversation forward.				
Participant, through his or her comments, demonstrates a depth of understanding of the text.				
Participant, through his or comments, demonstrates a depth of understanding for the question.				
Participant, through his or her comments, demonstrates he or she has actively listened to other participants.				
Participant offers clarification and follow-up that extends the conversation.				
Participant's remarks and comments refer to specific parts of the text.				
Participant is polite and respectful.				

Teacher comments: _____

_____

_____

_____

_____

_____

Student comments: _____

_____

_____

_____

_____

Prompt Title: _____

Interactive Notebook Pages

Directions: After reading, choose a quote and write it under the "Quote It" flap. Then write what you think is implied from this quote under the "The Quote Implies" flat. You are determining what you infer from the quote.

Quote
Page # _____

The Quote Implies

Quote
Page # _____

The Quote Implies

Instructions: Cut on the solid lines. Attach to your notebook and fold along the dashed lines.

Remember: An inference is a conclusion you reach based on context clues from <u>To Kill a Mockingbird</u> added to your own background knowledge and reasoning!!

Theme Development in TKAM. CCSS.RL.2

Over the course of the novel several themes emerged, choose one and cite details from <u>To Kill a Mockingbird</u> that show its development. Remember details include events, setting, dialogue, decisions and actions.

Theme:	When and how is the theme introduced?
	Cite details, including page numbers, about how and when the theme reemerges in the novel.
	In your opinion, whom does the theme effect the most?
	How is the theme fortified at the end of the novel?

Instructions: Cut along the solid lines and attach at the dotted line to your notebook. Write your thoughts under each box.

Details...Details...Details (and Key Events) CCSS. RL.R3
Plot Analysis

Analyze the events of <u>To Kill a Mockingbird</u>. Write the answer to the questions under each flap.

Issues, Issues: What is the first issue Scout faces?

Tension is Mounting: What conflicts result from the issues and who is effected?

Complicated and More Complicated: How do the characters escalate the conflict?

Tipping Point: What causes the tension to increase between the characters and the source of conflict?

The Climax: What event marks the more important part of the story. How do the characters react to the climax?

Resolution: How do the characters work to resolve the conflict after the climax?

Directions: Write down the types of conflicts under the corresponding flaps. Cut along the solid lines.

Types of Conflict

Scout	Scout	Scout	Scout
vs.	vs.	vs.	vs.
Man	Himself	Nature	Society

Character Conflict -- Boo: CCSS. RL.R3

Directions: Write down the types of conflicts under the corresponding flaps.
Cut along the solid lines.

Types of Conflict

Boo Radley	Boo Radley	Boo Radley	Boo Radley
vs.	vs.	vs.	vs.
Man	Himself	Nature	Society

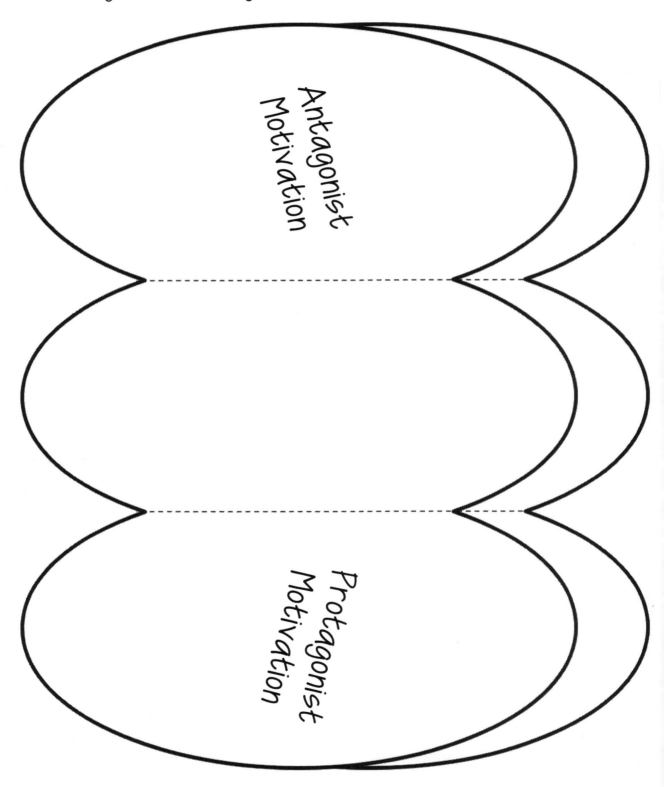

Protagonist: The main character
Antagonist: A character or force against which the main character struggles

Quotes

Directions: Write a quote from the text under the flap.

Quote 1		How does the quote propel the action of the story forward?
Quote 2		How does this quote expose Scout's character traits?
Quote 3		How does this quote cause Scout to take action?

Write quotes from the text that moves the story forward.

Analyze the quotes impact on the novel

Words, Words, Words... CCSS. ELA-Literacy.CCRA.R4

Directions: Cut along the solid black lines, fold on the dashed lines.

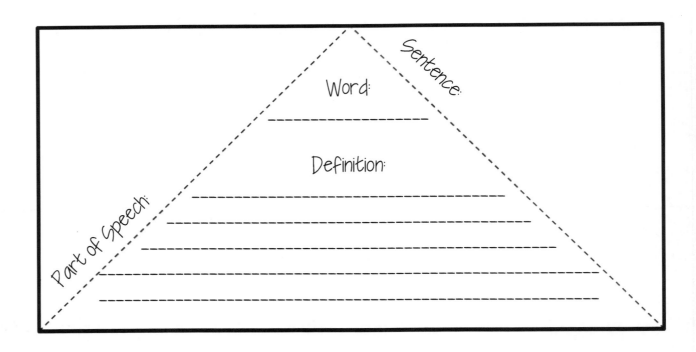

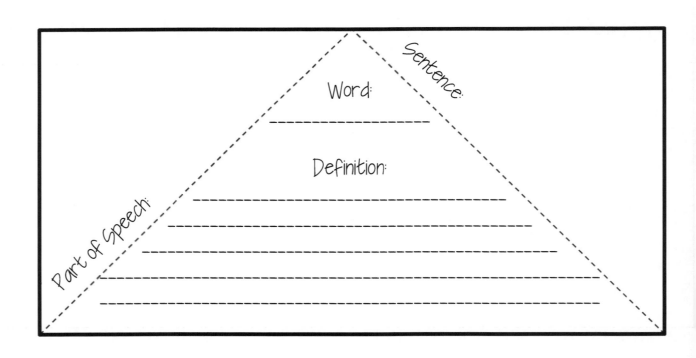

Metaphor		Imagery
Simile	Glue this side down	Personification
Static Character		Diction

Directions: Find examples of the following in the novel. Write the sound device in the middle box, the definition and example on your notebook page.

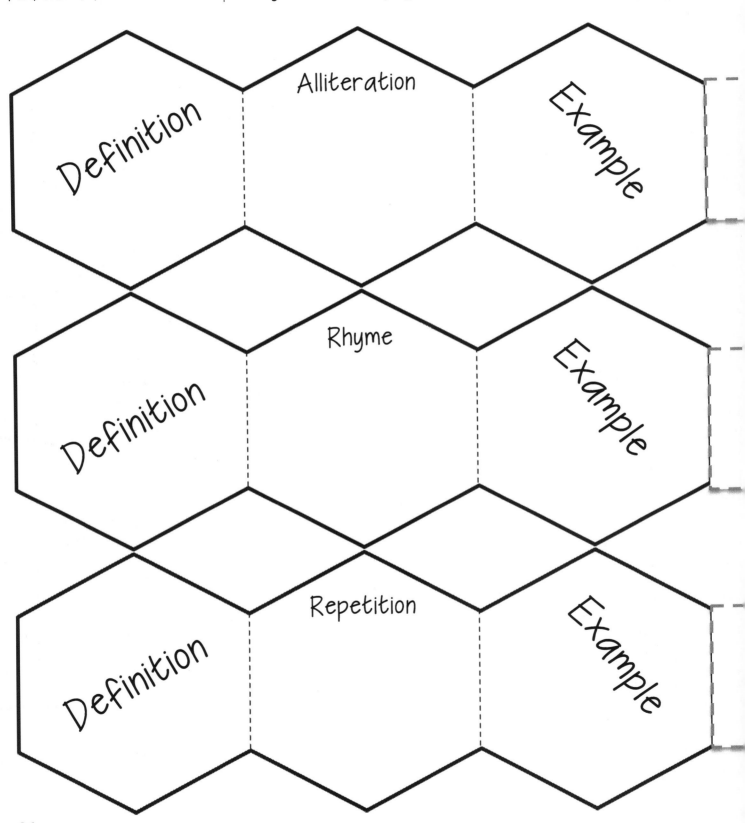

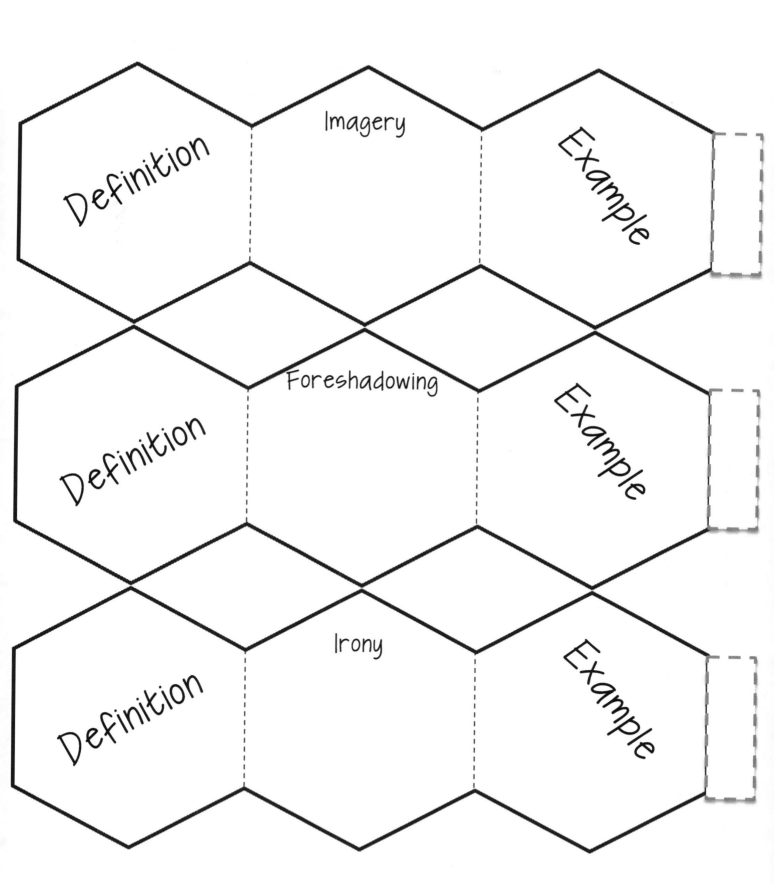

Definition

Imagery

Example

Definition

Foreshadowing

Example

Definition

Irony

Example

Directions: Analyze Twain's choice of words. For each word, give the literal meaning, what it connotes and how it influences the tone of the novel..

Word:

Meaning

Connotation

Impact

Word:

Meaning

Connotation

Impact

Theme and Structure of <u>To Kill a Mockingbird</u> – CCSS.ELA.Literacy.CCRA.R.5

How is the theme exposed through different passages?

Theme:

Passage:

Where is the theme first revealed in the novel?

Example of how the theme progresses through the novel.

Where and how does the theme come to its final conclusion?

Who is affected most by the theme development?

Write a different way this theme could have been resolved.

Directions: Cut along the solid lines. Write under the flaps..

To Kill a Mockingbird
Interactive Notebook
Universal Access

TO Kill a Mockingbird

By Harper Lee #103

Cover Design by: _____

Design and draw your own book cover

Critical Thinking Questions- #104

How does Atticus try in instill confidence into his children?

_____

_____

_____

_____

What would you do as Atticus?

_____

_____

_____

_____

Compare the failure of school to the failure of the justice system.

_____

_____

_____

_____

_____

Discuss how the author portrays Calpurnia.

_____

_____

_____

Describe one way Jem changes over the course of the novel?_____

About: TO Kill a Mockingbird
In My opinion... #105

What is your favorite part of the story? _____
_____
_____

Details why...

1. _____

_____

2. _____

_____

Who is your favorite character? _____
_____

Details why...

1. _____

_____

2. _____

_____

What is the main problem or conflict in the story? _____
_____

Details...

1. _____

_____

2. _____

_____

Name: _____ #: _____

TO Kill a Mockingbird
Constructed Response Questions - #106
Answer the following questions using complete sentences.

1. Describe the title in detail?_____

_____

_____

_____

_____

_____

_____

2. Use details to describe the one theme? _____

_____

_____

_____

_____

3. Describe Atticus in relation to the other characters in the novel. _____

_____

_____

_____

_____

4. Describe Ewell in relation to the other characters in the novel: _____

_____

_____

_____

Name: _____ #: _____

Story connectors
To Kill a Mockingbird- #107

In the beginning _____
_____
_____
_____

After that _____
_____
_____
_____

Later _____
_____
_____
_____

Just when _____
_____
_____
_____

At the end _____
_____
_____
_____

Name: _____   **#:** _____

character Analysis- #108

Character	Write three Character Traits for Each
Choose a Character	
Choose a Character	
Choose a Character	

SCOUT CHARACTER CONFLICTS - #109

Character Conflicts: A problem or struggle between two people, things or ideas.

What conflict developed as a result of Scout's actions?

_____

_____

_____

_____

How would you represent the actions of this conflict using the elements of the graphic novel? Draw it below.

sentence sorting -#110

Cut the sentence strips below and arrange them in the order they occur in
the story

TO Kill a Mockingbird

1) Sheriff Tate declared Bob Ewell's death an accident.

2) Jem and Scout go to school together in Maycomb, Alabama. On their way to school, they pass the
Radley house; it is a terrifying place to them, for it houses Boo Radley, who has been labeled a
lunatic. At the same time, their curiosity pushes them to try out ways to make Boo come out of the
house. Their overtures are, however, suppressed by Atticus who does not want them to torment
Boo.

3) Aunt Alexandra comes to live with the Finch's in Maycomb to give them a feminine influence. She
is prim and proper and mortified that the children are allowed to go back to the courtroom to hear
the verdict.

4) Scout's father Atticus is charged with defending a black man accused of raping the daughter of a
very poor young women named Mayella Ewell

5) The relation between the children and Boo Radley resurfaces at the end, when it is Boo who saves
them from imminent death at the hands of the vicious Bob Ewell. It is ultimately revealed that Boo is
not a lunatic, but a simple-minded person with failing health and a childish attachment for Scout and
Tom.

6) The case is lost simply because it was still impossible (despite statutory laws protecting them) for
a black man to attain victory over a white in the South. This amply reveals the deeply ingrained racial
prejudices still prevalent among the white society which cannot give an equal status to a black.

7) The story Atticus tells of the mockingbird highlights the theme of the novel. Atticus recounts that
it is considered a sin to kill a mockingbird because its singular purpose is to sing for the enjoyment of
others. Boo Radley and Tom Robinson are symbolically as harmless as the mockingbird. Through
Tom's death, the sin of killing a mockingbird comes to fruition.

sentence sorting to essay writing enrichment-#111

From Sentence Sorting to Essay Writing

GOAL: To gain a better understanding of what you read through reading and writing. To have an outline ready to go for an English/Language Arts writing assignment.

Directions:

Copy the template on the next page onto a transparency or use the computer generated sheet on a projector or document camera etc. Copy one blackline master per student.

Do a sample on the board and demonstrate the entire activity to the class – discuss the order of the sentence strips and copy them.

Check for understanding using think, speak and do strategies as you and your students write the essay together.

Review the sentence sorting activity as a group.

Work a modified scrip from the one herein to move from sentence sorting to essay writing.

Extension Assignment:

Have students choose a concept idea from the story.

Have students us the story to write their own sentence strips.

Re-pair up students with different partners and have them work self-created sentence strips.

Hand out another template and help students move from sentence strips to essay writing on their own.

For limited English proficient students and students who need extra help – you may want to do the assignment together – you on the board taking suggestions and them writing it down on their paper. Test and check as you help them to individualize their worksheet as you all move along together.

Hint to Motivate: Copy the template onto paper, laminate and have students use dry erase markers to construct their essays. When the rough draft is complete, have students peer edit and then copy their essays onto notebook paper. This saves time... helps with the editing process and engages students. There is something about dry erase markers and shiny surfaces that students love.

Name: _____ #: _____

From Sentence Sorting to Essay Writing
<u>To Kill a Mockingbird</u>

Paragraph 1: Write down the paragraph you created from your sentence strips.

1.	
2.	
3.	
4.	
5.	
6.	
7.	

Paragraph 2: Use one sentence from paragraph 1 as your topic sentence or "Main Idea" for this paragraph and another sentence from paragraph 1 as "Detail 2".

Main Idea:
Detail 1:
Supporting Fact:
Detail 2:
Supporting Fact:
Concluding Sentence:

Paragraph 3: Use one sentence from paragraph 1 as your topic sentence or "Main Idea" for this paragraph and another sentence from paragraph 1 as "Detail 2".

Main Idea:	
Detail 1:	
Supporting Fact:	
Detail 2:	
Supporting Fact:	
Concluding Sentence:	

Paragraph 4: Use one sentence from paragraph 1 as your topic sentence or "Main Idea" for this paragraph and another sentence from paragraph 1 as "Detail 2".

Main Idea:	
Detail 1:	
Supporting Fact:	
Detail 2:	
Supporting Fact:	
Concluding Sentence:	

Paragraph 5 – Conclusion; Use your "Thesis Statement" from paragraph 1 as your **main idea** for this concluding paragraph.

Thesis Statement:
Detail 1:
Supporting Fact:
Detail 2:
Supporting Fact:
Concluding Sentence:

Quick Write Compare and Contrast - #115

Compare Scout with Dill.

Scout	Similarities	Dill

Summarize the results from your graphic organizers.

_____

_____

_____

_____

_____

About the Author - #116

Nelle Harper Lee was born on April 28, 1926, in Monroeville, Alabama. She completed the manuscript for her Pulitzer Prize-winning best-seller *To Kill a Mockingbird* in 1959. She was the childhood friend of Truman Capote.

Lee had four brothers and sisters of which she was the youngest. Growing up as a tomboy in a small town, Lee is very much like her protagonist Scout. Her father was a lawyer, a member of the Alabama state legislature and also owned part of the local newspaper. For most of Lee's life, her mother suffered from mental illness, rarely leaving the house. It is believed that she may have had bipolar disorder.

Compare and contrast Scout with Harper Lee.

Name: _____ **#:** _____

Story Summary - #117

Please summarize the following.

Character:

Plot:

Setting:

Name: _____ **#:** _____

Character Changes- #118

Please summarize the following.

Character	At the **beginning** of the story...	At the **end** of the story...
Scout		
Jem		
Boo Radley		

Name: _____ #: _____

Text to Text— #119
Connecting Fiction Texts

To Kill a
Mockingbird

_____
Book Title

How can you connect these two texts?

Name: _____ #: _____

My Thoughts While Reading **TO Kill a Mockingbird**- #120

Please write down any thoughts you have while we/you read the story..

My Thoughts	Page # Related

Name: _____ **#:** _____

Inferring Character Feelings - #121

Character: _____

How do they feel? _____

_____

_____

Evidence from Text to Support MY Thinking: _____

_____

_____

_____

Character: _____

How do they feel? _____

_____

_____

Evidence from Text to Support MY Thinking: _____

_____

_____

_____

Name: _____ **#:** _____

Cause and Effect- #122

What is the cause and effect of Scout's innocence in relation to the racial remarks she makes while narrating the story.

Cause – Because of this......_____

_____

_____

_____

_____

Effect – This happens......_____

_____

_____

_____

_____

Name: _____ #: _____

Compare and Contrast Atticus and Scout-- #128

Atticus

Scout

Similarities

_____
_____
_____
_____
_____

Think, Question and Analyze-#124

Name one symbol of the novel:

_____
_____
_____
_____

Theme of <u>To Kill a Mockingbird</u>:

_____
_____
_____
_____
_____
_____
_____
_____

Theme: A theme is the underlying meaning of a literary work. A theme may be stated or implied.

One question I have is: _____

_____
_____
_____
_____
_____
_____
_____
_____
_____

Most interesting thought I have about the book: _____

_____
_____
_____
_____
_____

One word to describe the book:

_____

Name: _____ **#:** _____

TO Kill a MOCKingbird Report Card #25

Grade	Grade and Comments
Setting	
Main Character	
Supporting Characters	
Plot	
Symbols	
Beginning	
Conflict	
Ending	

<u>To Kill a Mockingbird</u> Book Review #126

Things I liked about this book: _____

_____

_____

_____

_____

Things I would change about this book: _____

_____

_____

_____

Would you recommend this book and why or why not:_____

_____

_____

_____

_____

Star rating...

☆☆☆☆☆

Signed: _____

Lights, Camera, Action – #127

Describe your favorite scene from <u>To Kill a Mockingbird</u> and then draw it in four panels.

_____

_____

_____

_____

_____

_____

_____

_____

_____

_____

_____

_____

_____

_____

_____

_____

Text A Friend What You Predict Will Happen Next
Chapter-by-Chapter 128

Instructions: Cut out the phone and past it in your Interactive Literature Notebook. Cut out a faceplate for each chapter to predict what will happen next. Don't forget to make it look like a chat conversation.

Text A Friend What You Predict Will Happen Next
Chapter-by-Chapter

Chapter ____

Chapter ____

Chapter ____

Chapter ____

chapter _ _ _ _

chapter _ _ _ _

chapter _ _ _ _

chapter _ _ _ _

chapter _ _ _ _

chapter _ _ _ _

Rubrics and Answers

Rubric for ALL Constructed Response Questions #132

The constructed-response questions of the new 21st Century assessments ask students to produce his or her own answers to questions rather than selecting the correct response from a list. Some constructed-response questions require students to write short compositions – much like some of the questions in this unit. All constructed response questions can be corrected using the rubric below —quickly and easily – as long as we – the teachers – understand the content inside and out.

Remember what the objective of constructed response questions is:
"Constructed-response items for reading provide students with an opportunity to demonstrate basic understanding of passages and to reflect on what has been read in order to respond and create personal meaning. Constructed-response items also reinforce the concept of reading for a variety of reasons, especially to solve a problem or answer a question and learn about diverse perspectives, cultures and issues in traditional and contemporary literature."

Again, this rubric may be used for all constructed response questions in this handbook.

Rubric
Wow! Really, you carry around enough rubrics to use this with EACH question. Are you totally insane? No, no and no again. Just keep the number system in your head as you go through the questions.

Score	Description	Score Tally
4	Response answered the question, relates to the reading and student has a grasp of the main story element (s) applicable.	
3	Response answers the question, relates to the reading and student has a grasp of the main story element(s) applicable – but complete sentences were not used and there are problems with spelling and/or grammar.	
2	Response provides a partial answer with limited, incomplete or partially correct information	
1	Response is minimal or vague.	
0	No or incorrect response.	

Name: _____

Rubric for Constructed Response _____

Please attach assignment.

Score	Description	Score Tally
4	Response answered the question, relates to the reading and student has a grasp of the main story element (s) applicable.	
3	Response answers the question, relates to the reading and student has a grasp of the main story element(s) applicable – but complete sentences were not used and there are problems with spelling and/or grammar.	
2	Response provides a partial answer with limited, incomplete or partially correct information	
1	Response is minimal or vague.	
0	No or incorrect response.	

Teacher Comments: _____

_____

_____

_____

_____

_____

Student Comments: _____

_____

_____

_____

_____

Answers

Page 16: 1d 2c 3c 4b 5a 6c 7c 8d
Page 19: 1a 2c 3a 4d 5a 6d 7a 8c
Page 22: 1a 2d 3b 4d 5b 6d 7b 8b
Page 24: 1b 2c 3a 4c 5a 6b 7d 8b
Page 27: 1a 2c 3b
Page 30: 1a 2d 3b 4d 5a 6b 7a
Page 44: 1a 2c 3c 4c 5d 6b 7a
Page 47: 1c 2b 3c 4c 5b 6a 7d
Page 50: 1c 2d 3d 4a 5a 6b 7a
Page 53: 1c 2d 3d 4b 5a 6a 7a
Page 56: 1c 2a 3b 4d 5a – TFFTTTTT
Page 59: 1c 2d 3d 4c 5c 6b 7b 8c
Page 62: 1c 2b 3a 4c 5a 6b 7c 8b
Page 65: 1c 2b 3c 4c 5a 6c 7a 8c
Page 68: 1b 2d 3c 4c 5a 6a 7b 8c

#110: 2, 4, 3, 6, 5, 1, 7

For student samples of each activity in this novel unit, please email elizabeth@luckyjenny.com.

For more interactive Novel Units, novels and free curriculum visit www.luckyjenny.com -- and check back often – we are always adding to our inventory.

Borders by Creative Clips' fabulous Krista Wallden: http://www.teacherspayteachers.com/Store/Krista-Wallden

Printed in Great Britain
by Amazon